To: Betty, we had some experiences at the C-E, some good some awful. Enjoy the book, it's meant to entertain as well as inform.

— Joe Ritz

I Never Looked for My Mother

And Other Regrets of a Journalist

By

Joseph P. Ritz

10-Digit ISBN 1-59113-879-5
13-Digit ISBN 978-1-59113-879-2

Printed in the United States of America.

Booklocker.com, Inc.
2006

I Never Looked for My Mother

And Other Regrets of a Journalist

By

Joseph P. Ritz

Introduction

This book was begun at the suggestion of one of my children, who thought I should write down some of the stories I had been telling at gatherings of family and friends. After some thought, I agreed. If they are going to tell stories about me after I'm gone, I want to be sure they get them right.

It has since evolved. It has become less of a story about an unusual childhood and the capricious couple who pretended to be my parents. More space has been given to telling of stories about and comments on journalism, particularly newspaper journalism, as I remember it practiced during a lifetime in the profession. I have worked on or have had stories published in newspapers from Seattle to New York City. I have written more than ten million words for publication or production in my lifetime. Most of them were written on old mechanical typewriters, one of which is on the jacket cover of this book. I have tales to tell, many of them funny, others a bit shocking.

Having written so many words, it's not surprising that some of them have been applauded with professional awards. In the mid-1960s, I contributed to a newspaper series entitled, *The Road to Integration,* which won a Pulitzer Prize. I am proud of an award from the New York State AFL-CIO For outstanding achievements and contributions on behalf of working men and women and of receiving the Byline Award from my alma mater, Marquette University.

Since they learned to talk, my grandchildren, at the half-in-jest urging of their parents, have called me Grumpy.

And so I dedicate this book to my children and grandchildren.

Chapter 1

Putting on the Ritz

I was born a bastard and I have remained one throughout my life. I became a journalist. A bastard in the vulgar sense of being unpopular or disagreeable is not a serious handicap in that sometimes unpleasant and too often poorly paid profession.

Most of us have watched movies or television shows portraying journalists as drunks, headline-hunting sadists, crime solvers, self-seekers and lady-killers, but never have I seen one portrayed as a comic, a role both reporters and editors sometimes inadvertently play. Never, for instance, have I seen a film showing a reporter accidentally plunging his hand into three-foot high, uncut 100th anniversary cake at a formal dinner as one Buffalo Courier-Express reporter did when I worked there later in my career.

For the most part, newspaper stories are written hurriedly by an overburdened journalist with no time for reflection or rewriting. As a result, sometimes reporters and their editors are embarrassed by what appears in print. I have in mind a correction of a story when I worked on New Haven paper. The original story was about a local man who had been hospitalized on returning from an African safari.

Thousands of readers the next morning read the following complete account:

Yesterday's edition incorrectly stated that John Mitchell has returned to his home on Orange Avenue. Mitchell, who was bitten by a dragon, is recovering in New Haven Hospital

Startling as the statement was to readers, given time to reflect, the reporter might have added that the dragon in the story was the African name for a particular insect. Or, perhaps, she did and the sentence was cut for space.

There are many stories told among newsmen about the foibles and eccentrics of their fellow journalists. When I began my career as a journalist, the profession was still peopled by older reporters who lacked a college degree and pounded out stories with two fingers on manual typewriters. They were often colorful people and the best of them could write a good story. The lack of a degree often meant that reporters instinctively wrote in the lively vernacular of the mass of their readers. They wrote about, instead of the wordy and awkward in reference to. They knew verbs make a story fly. Fleeing men or women ran, they didn't escape on foot; they hoped, they weren't hopeful. Today, newspapers too often are less readable and interesting because reporters and editors increasingly use the dull and awkwardly worded language of official reports and bureaucrats. Even the atrocious and nonsensical description of preowned rather than used car is creeping into news stories. If a car isn't owned why not just take it?

And with important news instantly available to the average person over the airwaves or the Internet, the major original purpose of a newspaper to provide news of an event before the reader is aware of it has gone. In fact it began to be supplanted nearly 100 years ago when Pittsburgh radio station KDKA announced the news that Warren G. Harding had beaten James Cox for presidency of the United States. Long before their newspaper is delivered, people know that airplanes have struck the Twin Towers, that a hurricane has devastated New Orleans, a local or national figure has been elected or that a celebrity has been convicted or found innocent by a jury. And yet newspapers often read as though they are surprising readers with news that everyone has heard over and over.

The value of newspapers today lies in uncovering facts and details that otherwise would never be known by the public and writing them so they are easy to read. The news magazines *Time, Newsweek, U.S. News & World Report* have gained audiences of millions by doing just that. For daily newspapers to do something similar requires more time than many editors today are willing or able to give a reporter as the size of the editorial staffs have decreased. The emphasis is still too often on the misplaced idea of getting the story first because that's the way it has always been done.

When I began my career as a journalist, newspaper offices were noisy and smoke-filled, unlike many today that often are hushed and peopled with quiescent figures in business suits and dresses.

One of the old-time reporters at the *Courier-Express* was Dan George (not his real name). Dan was a stubby man with a round face, part of which was adorned by a large pair of wire-rimmed glasses. His hair, what you could see of it under the hat he usually wore both outside and inside, was nearly white, as was his large mustache.

He had worked for several papers in various parts of the country before landing at the C-E many years before I arrived. His talent as a writer was limited and so the city desk assigned him to write obituaries and, when pressed, to review lesser musical performances when no one else was available.

The paper had a policy of publishing obituaries only of persons who had achieved some measure, however small, of prominence.

Dan made himself the arbiter of what would be published. Since he didn't like to write a lot of obituaries, he set the bar at a high level and demanded that funeral directors and sometimes members of the family of the dead person clear it.

"Madam, what has your husband ever done to merit an obituary?" was typical of Dan's challenges to wives of men who had died within the last 48 hours and who were bold or foolish enough to call the paper directly to ask for an obituary. Once he was overheard asking a very recent widow: "You mean your husband did nothing for twenty years!"

Dan was from time to time assigned to cover a meeting of a town board in one of the several suburbs around Buffalo. The assignments ceased because Dan would at times become enraged at a proposal being debated. Although he wasn't a resident of the town and reporters are commanded to be neutral observers, Dan would rise from his seat, and, in a loud voice, add his opinions to the debate.

Reporters who worked with Dan tell of the time he was assigned to get a photograph from the family of a prominent businessman who had unexpectedly died. The family lived some 20 miles distant and the deadline for the main edition of the paper was nearing. Dan was asked by the city editor to speed to the deceased man's home, get the photo and return post haste.

An hour passed without sign of Dan or the photograph. An hour and one-half went by. The city editor's phone rang. It was a state policeman calling.

"Have you got a reporter by the name of Dan George?"

"Yes, but officer, if he's been speeding we would appreciate it if you could please release him. The paper will pay the fine. He has something we must have for the next edition."

"Speeding?" The trooper's voice sounded surprised. "He was traveling under 40 miles an hour on the Thruway. We were afraid he was going to be rear ended."

***

Those are among the tales I tell at gatherings of friends. They are memories of things that happened long after I became of age. To get back to the beginning of this book, I described myself as a bastard. Not in temperament, but in the first meaning of the word as an "illegitimate child." I can tell you nothing about my mother. We met briefly and said our painful goodbyes in the Chicago hospital in which I was born. I do not know her name.

To be a good journalist requires asking a lot of questions about a wide range of topics. At an early age I began silently questioning whether the persons who were raising me were my parents. That eventually led to more questions about my background: Who were my parents? What kind of people were they? What talents or inclinations have I inherited?

Part of me has always feared the answers.

I have only a few memories of my early years in Chicago. I have a vivid memory of a large neon sign that featured an animated Dutch girl chasing dirt with a broom. I have vague memories of a red wagon, of fighting on the sidewalk with other children, of feeling the weight of several boys on top of me, of taking a toy engine down to the locomotive shops where my foster father worked and being made much of by the men, who laughed and talked to me. I remember riding on a white horse led by a boy.

I was taken to the Chicago World's Fair, but the only thing I remember from it are scenes from a black and white movie of *Alice in*

Wonderland in which a woman's swanlike neck kept growing longer and then shorter, very puzzling to a young boy.

I saw Babe Ruth play a few times when the White Sox and the Yankees met on a ladies matinee day and my foster mother took me to the game, but I do not remember the Babe.

As a journalist I was to encounter many people as famous or as near famous as the Babe.

Newspaper reporters are mostly onlookers. We are usually kept at a distance from the inner workings of a government. We rarely see a crime committed. We seldom become close friends with political figures or entertainers, nor should we.

But a reporter does interview prominent people from time to time, and in that manner comes into closer contact with them than does the public.

Of all the national political figures I have encountered in 40 years as a journalist, Harry S Truman had the most natural and unforced rapport with ordinary people on a face-to-face basis. Harry Truman who looked like a man who had spent his life at a desk adding up small sums; a man who any movie or stage director worth his salt would have cast as the manager of a small bank branch in a rural community; a man who spoke in a voice almost devoid of dramatic inflection and made awkward gestures with his arms. On television he appeared stiff and dull. I would not have voted for him had he run for reelection in 1952. I was astonished to find him quick-witted and full of vitality in person.

I came in contact with Truman when I was a young reporter for the *New Haven Journal-Courier.* He had left office five years before and now spending three days at Yale under a Chubb Fellowship, which is intended to afford students an opportunity to meet and talk with world political leaders over a period of several days.

When he arrives at Yale, Truman appears a little cowed by its intellectual reputation. He admits he is apprehensive about his visit. But, he had been president of the United States, the most powerful nation in the world at the end of a war that would change society nearly everywhere in the world and he knows he has a major role in its history.

"I never went to college," he admits to the students and faculty in his first appearance before them. "If I had, I would never have been admitted to a place like Yale University. But I had people who went to Yale to advise me, people like Dean Acheson. They gave me good advice and information, but no matter how good their advice was and how much knowledge they had, I was the one who made the final decisions, and I stand by those decisions."

Truman's habit of taking morning half-hour walks continues now that he is ex-president, continues while he is in New Haven. He invites anyone interested, including reporters, to join him at 7:30 a.m. on walks around the Yale grounds.

He goes at a brisk pace from the master's house at Timothy Dwight College, where he is staying. He is surrounded by about 30 students, detectives and journalists. A radio broadcaster announces his progress.

At that time, ex-presidents were not protected by the Secret Service. New Haven's Democratic mayor, Richard Lee, has ordered squads of police to provide protection for Truman.

"Mr. Truman, what do you think of all this heavy police protection the mayor has given you?" a reporter asks the ex-president at his news conference. It is a question meant to embarrass Truman. There is no good answer. He can reply that he doesn't approve of the phalanx of police around him and thereby embarrass the major and his host, Yale University. Or, he can say he likes the protection and cause many citizens of New Haven to say, "Who does he think he is? An ex-president, after all. Why should we taxpayers be paying for his protection?"

Truman doesn't hesitate to respond. In his soft, flat Missouri drawl he replies, "When ah was president ah don't think ah did anything bad enough that someone's gonna shoot me."

The response brings an admiring laugh from the press.

Truman gives every impression he is enjoying the conference, despite some mean-spirited questions. My perception is confirmed after Truman leaves New Haven when I interview Thomas G. Bergin, dean of Yale's Timothy Dwight College, and his wife, in whose three-story house Truman and Acheson had stayed.

"Truman came back from the press conference invigorated," the dean tells me. "He said he enjoyed it. It reminded him of the days he was president."

My experience with Adali Stevenson, who was a Chubb fellow for five days the following year, was not as pleasant, but it was revealing. Truman had a common touch in person, but was stiff and didactic on television.

Stevenson was comfortable and witty on the small screen, but in New Haven he appeared aloof and superior.

Truman liked people and relished the give and take in answering questions from reporters. Stevenson appeared to accept a press conference as a necessary, but unwanted chore in which he condescended to answer questions from persons less knowledgeable than he.

My view, however, may be colored by Stevenson's giving me a scolding over what I think was a perfectly proper political question.

I wanted to know if he was interested in again running for president in the 1960 election race the following year, now that he would not again have to run against Eisenhower to whom he had twice lost. He answered urbanely that he had been given the rare privilege of running for the nation's highest office twice and he had no plans to run a third time.

"But would you accept a draft?" I asked.

He bristled. His body became taller and stiff. He looked at me sternly as though I had made an improper sexual proposal.

"I don't expect to be drafted." Then he dressed me down. "I don't regard that as a question I should be asked at this occasion," he said. ÒI didn't come here for political reasons. I'm here to meet with the students at Yale. What you asked was not a proper question."

"No, that's not a proper question," a minion from the Yale public information office echoed. "Mr. Stevenson is here as a private citizen. He should not be asked that kind of political questions."

Hell, if he were only a private citizen, I wouldn't have asked if he still wanted to run for president.

Truman was the only ex-U.S. president I covered as a reporter. I did have close contact with Richard Nixon on a couple of occasions when he was vice president. The first was when I was newly out of college and working as a radio news writer in Flint, Michigan.

That was in 1955, when Flint's auto plants were attracting workers from all over the nation and the city was celebrating its 150th birthday. General Motors, which had its origins in the city, gave truckloads of money and used its political influence to make the event memorable. Charlie Wilson, former chairman of GM, was secretary of defense. Postmaster Arthur Summerfield was not only a prominent Republican nationally; he owned the largest Chevrolet dealership in Flint.

I suspect that had much to do with Vice President Nixon's coming to Flint for the celebration. General Motors went to great lengths to keep the press comfortable. Besides the usual lunches and dinners, a 24-hour bar was set up in a room of the Hotel Durant at which the media could drink for free. A new Buick and a driver were at the call of every journalist.

Nixon spent only a day in Flint—time enough to visit one of the auto plants and shake hands with workers and ride in the lead car of the parade, during which he received far less applause and waves from the crowd than the singer and movie actress, Dinah Shore, riding in the second car with her current husband, fading movie star and former cowboy, George Montgomery. It was not a coincidence that GM was the chief sponsor of Dinah Shore's television show.

I stood a few feet from Nixon as he shook hands with the workers at Buick Plant #2. He didn't have the warmth of Vice President Hubert Humphrey and many of the other national political figures and even some of the local politicians I was to later cover. Watching Nixon trying to be friendly with the workers, made me think of an ambitious new junior executive meeting the help for the first time. There was an attitude of forced friendliness mingled with a trace of awkwardness on the part of both the vice president and the workers.

The second occasion was when I left journalism to take a short-lived fling at public relations as assistant news director at Fordham University in NYC. That experience taught me I didn't have the desire or the personality to succeed at a job where writing was secondary to meeting and greeting -- skills at which I was then too shy and socially awkward to succeed at an institution that considered itself to be the Harvard of Catholic universities. I believed then and still believe that trying to tell the truth to the public is a higher calling than beating the drum for an institution, no matter how worthy.

Nixon was running for president against John F. Kennedy when I was at Fordham. At that time Fordham was, for the most part, a Republican island in the Democratic sea of New York City and Nixon was invited to speak on campus.

The invitation enraged Bobby Kennedy, who complained to the school administration.

Your brother was also invited to speak, he was told.

"You know that as a Catholic candidate for president he couldn't speak at a Catholic institution. It would add fuel to the anti-Catholic sentiment," Bobby responded.

So Nixon became the only candidate to speak at Fordham during the campaign. Seeing him perform close up did nothing to change my earlier opinion of him as an ambitious junior executive.

It's not unusual for a politician to be angered by something a journalist has written. It's rare to be publicly scolded by someone in public office at a press conference. It happened to me only twice. The first time was the brush up with Adali Stevenson. It was to happen once again when Nelson Rockefeller was governor of New York and soon to be President Ford's vice president.

It came about as a result of a misunderstanding.

I was a reporter on the *Buffalo Courier-Express* covering a press conference over the governor's plan to assure that significant numbers of blacks would be hired for well-paying construction jobs to create a new State University of Buffalo campus. A sizable number of civil rights groups show up to voice their demands for racial quotas that would assure a greater percentage of blacks are hired. The meeting starts disintegrating into an unruly shouting match.

One of the Rockefeller aides asks me to help the governor exit gracefully.

9

"You're the senior reporter here. Would you ask the governor a question and then after he answers, give a sort of 'thank you, Mr. President,' so we can get out of here?"

I agree. I have exhausted the questions for which my readers needed answers. I ask some simple, innocuous query from the front row and, as the governor responds, turn around to other members of the press to tell them we are being asked to leave as soon as Rockefeller finishes his answer.

What the governor sees is me turning my back to him as he is speaking. He blows his top.

"Listen you," he says, shaking his finger at me. "You asked a question. Now I think you should turn around and listen to its answer."

I don't fault him for his indignation and his admonishment. I didn't get a chance to apologize, and under the circumstances I could not explain what I had been doing. I hope that sometime during his trip back to the airport one of his aides told him the purpose of my question.

The national politician with whom I had the most personal contact was Jack Kemp. My youngest daughter, Margaret, a white water rafting guide and ski instructor in Vail, disclosed to her friends, when Kemp was Republican vice presidential candidate in 1988, that she had sat on his lap as a baby. At the time Kemp was our congressman and she had been crying and disruptive in his office as he was talking to my wife and I.

I had written a profile of Kemp when he was president of the American Football Players Association, which he had co-founded. He seemed a bit uncomfortable with my description of him as a labor leader, but we got along fine. When *The Courier-Express* folded in September of 1982, Kemp was the only politician who actively tried to find me a job in Washington.

I covered several of Kemp's speeches and activities when he was congressman. I remember one event in particular. I was assigned to write a story about Kemp presenting a football to a grade school student in a ceremony at one of the local parks. After the presentation, Kemp, who had first gained fame as an AFL championship quarterback for the Buffalo Bills, threw a few soft passes to the boy before leaving.

When he left, the boy looked downcast. I offered to throw him a pass. His face brightened. I grabbed the football and threw a pass to -- a sewer opening that a park employee had just uncovered.

Chapter 2

I Never Knew My Mother But She Was Beautiful

It has taken a long lifetime to understand what I owe both to my own unknown natural mother and to the two unfortunate persons who raised me.

The mismatched couple who adopted me was often confused, little educated, sometimes abusive and impulsive, afraid and prejudiced and full of longings that were never filled. They were also regular churchgoers, generous within their very limited means, as honest as the next person, hard working and determined to survive. In other words, common people.

Most children are stuck with the parents they have. Many children from time to time hope and believe they are adopted. But for them it is just wishful thinking.

We may fight it, deny it and resent it, but most of us become our parents when we reach middle age. Not knowing who you are likely to become is like being given a wrapped gift and being unable to open it until you are 45.

I assume, without any evidence beyond what I can detect in my body and in my sinful inclinations that my mother was beautiful and my father was a faithless rouge.

When I was a teenager I used to search my face in the mirror looking for clues that would tell what my parents looked like. The evidence is that one parent, or both, had dark brunette hair and blue eyes and a fair skin that blistered after a day in the sun every May and was sprinkled with freckles early in life. There is some red hair in my background. I noticed a few strands of it in my otherwise dark brown beard when I was a young man.

Depending on my mood or what movie I had recently seen when I was growing up, my father was a famous baritone appearing regularly in the world's leading stages. Or, rouge that he was, he made his way as an undercover investigator, handsome with an Irish face, a young Ronald Reagan type of guy with an easy laugh and a quick trigger finger. Or, he was a major leaguer, a Celtic Joe DiMaggio who led the league in home runs and batting averages. Unless, he was fighting for the heavyweight championship of the world or fighting outlaws out west, the quickest draw between Dodge City and Sacramento, a John Wayne/Gary Cooper type of guy who spoke with measured words that instilled fear into the hearts of the cruel and wicked, the cheats, the liars, the bullies of the world.

My mother was always young and beautiful in my imagination. Her long, glossy, dark hair flowed in loose curls down her back until it ended just below her shoulder blades. She had high, prominent cheekbones and a mouth slightly smaller than average that frequently broadened into a mirthful grin. Her voice was soft and musical. She loved singing. She was quick to dance and eager to play.

What I have of her from the South Chicago hospital in which I was born is my face and ample six-foot body and a cracked and torn brown rubber Lindbergh doll with part of the head missing. It hangs on the wall of the den where I am writing this.

THE details of my adoption are sketchy and come from a very unreliable source -- my foster mother.

She herself was unable to have children. But her husband was determined to override God's better judgment. I think also each was looking for an ally in their many violent quarrels.

We lived in a world of make believe. They pretended I was their natural child. I pretended to be unaware I wasn't their son.

I was given away by my mother only a few days after my birth, but my awareness that the unhappy, quarreling couple I knew as Father and Mother weren't my real parents, though unspoken, lingered in a corner of my mind as long as I can remember. And then there were hints about my status in the small family throughout my early life.

If my foster mother is to be believed, her husband, Joseph E. Ritz, had gone alone to St. Francis Hospital in search of a son. On learning he was Catholic, married and had a job, hospital authorities gave me to him and his wife. They apparently believed that was sufficient to assure my future well being physically and spiritually.

"They said at the hospital that if we didn't take you then, it would be harder for us to adopt once an agency got involved," my foster mother told me when I at last confronted her with my unwavering belief I was not her natural son. I was 18 and had finished high school six months earlier.

"A banker and his wife, very wealthy people, wanted you very bad, but they wouldn't let them adopt you because they weren't Catholic."

Being raised by a wealthy Protestant couple wouldn't have been that bad, I thought.

My natural mother was said to be Irish-American, blue-eyed, dark-haired, pretty and 26 at the time I was born. She was the sister of not one, but two priests, "one so high up in the church it would kill him if he knew of your existence." At the time of my birth, she was said to be working as a housekeeper at the rectory where her brother was pastor. It was not a place where an illegitimate child could be raised. I would have been living evidence that a significant mortal sin had been committed by the sister of priests who preached chastity before marriage.

I was told my mother sometimes came to a park to see me when I was being wheeled in carriage. It fits the image I have of her. I do not remember her.

I think I was six or seven when I first became convinced I was adopted. For one thing, I didn't look like either of my parents. My "father" was of Sicilian blood, although he tried to pass himself off as a Frenchman. He was born Joseph Rizzi in Blairsville Intersection, Pa., which was a hamlet of less than 100 persons surrounding a water tower used to refill the boilers on steam engines on the Pennsylvania Railroad. Both his parents were poor Sicilian immigrants. The year of his birth was 1894, the same as my foster mother's.

He went to public school through the fifth grade before dropping out to help support the family. His lack of education was not at all unusual for adults in the period. In 1940 only two of five adults in the U.S. had an eighth grade education, only one in four were high school graduates.

He was proud of having gone to work at an early age. He often told me of it, boasting of putting all his paychecks in his mother's lap.

When he was a teenager he and his three brothers sought to avoid prejudice against the Italians by informally changing their surname to Ritz. The name and its variations had recently become part of American slang for something swanky, which, I imagine, they considered themselves. I don't think they had heard of the Paris hotel from which the name came.

So I was, in effect, named after a foreign hotel. Many years later my wife and I are visiting Paris and we try to enter the Ritz Hotel. I would have breezed right into the lobby, but my wife, overawed by the exclusiveness and fame of the place, is hesitant and hangs back.

The doorman takes a quick look at us and asks if we are guests.

"No. But we want to see the dinner menu," I say, attempting to look like someone who was accustomed to shelling out the price of a new Renault for dinner for two and a bottle of the best champagne in the house.

He assesses us coldly. "I'm sorry monsieur, but only guests may enter," he replies, barring our way.

I thought of telling him I was named after the hotel and showing him my American Express card, but I suspect he would not have been impressed.

The Rizzis became the Ritzs after they left Pennsylvania and followed the railroad tracks to Chicago to look for work.

One of the brothers, Sal, soon got involved in organized crime and one day disappeared like Jimmy Hoffa, never to be heard of again. I never learned the details. It was not often talked about even at the funerals of members of my father's family.

I recall the wake of a distant relative at which several of the men got into a heated discussion about whether the police had been justified in shooting the deceased while he was running from the scene of a burglary. It was important to them, and at the time as a young boy the discussion didn't seem at all odd or unusual. It may have been then that I first heard about the mysterious disappearance of my father's brother.

The other three Ritz brothers got menial jobs on the railroad. Some time in this pre-World War I period, my father married before a justice of the peace. The marriage lasted only a brief time and when the war broke out in 1917, 23-year-old Joseph Ernest Ritz enlisted in the U.S. Army, eventually becoming first sergeant in an infantry line company. He went to France. He sometimes talked vaguely about the horrors of trench warfare, but he never talked specifically about the fighting. Like most children, I didn't know enough to ask the right questions.

Returning to Chicago after the war, he got a job as a boilermaker and fought in amateur boxing matches as a middleweight. During this period he met my foster mother, who was working as a telegraph operator for Western Union. They were married in St. Mary's Catholic Church in Chicago's loop in 1922.

She married him, she told me several times, "because I was so big. (She was five feet eleven, large-boned, fair-skinned and fleshy. He was five seven, medium build and walnut skinned with black hair parted close to the middle and heavy black eyebrows above dark brown eyes.)

"I was 28. Who else was I going to get?"

Other times she said she married him because he looked like Rudolph Valentino," the swarthy, silent screen idol she and so many millions of young women adored. (To attract women, after Valentino starred in *The Sheik,* college-age men began wearing baggy-style Valentino pants.)

I think he married her because she was half Irish. He was ashamed of being Italian and never publicly acknowledged it. I can understand his feelings. In parochial school when I was a boy our heroes were Irish: Pat O'Brien in *The Fighting 69th,* Spencer Tracy as Father Flanagan in *Boys Town,* Bing Crosby, "The Fighting Irish" of Notre Dame. St. Patrick's Day was a school holiday. Columbus Day was not. Those who were Irish were proud of it. Those who were not, wished they were.

To my father, used to going to confession to Irish pastors, kissing the ring of Irish bishops, voting for Irish politicians and seeing Irish

Table of Contents

faces in the ads, the Irish were a superior race of people. It was a belief the woman he married never let him forget.

I think the stronger of the two reasons my mother gave for marrying my legal father was that he looked like Valentino.

She had a mania for the movies. Even during the Depression, when we had little money and she had to pawn her wedding ring, she took me to movies every weekend at one of the second run movie houses in Canton.

For a quarter, we would see the feature attraction, a B movie -- usually a western or a detective story -- a cartoon, previews of coming attractions, a newsreel and sometimes a Robert Bentley comic short or a Pete Smith feature portraying such remarkable talents as a pool shark who could sink a rack of balls with one cue shot.

Once, when my father was in the hospital, my mother and I went to two movie houses in one afternoon watching nearly six hours of movies without a commercial break.

But watching movies with my mother could be embarrassing for a young boy. She had a very tentative grasp on reality and the line between the real and the fictional was often erased in her mind. She firmly believed that Sherlock Holmes was a real person and I didn't have the heart or the courage to try to disillusion her. She was a woman who abhorred displays of affection and she didn't care for love stories, but she would shriek with terror during a mystery, often warning the figures on the screen of dangers of which they were seemingly unaware.

But I was most apprehensive when the newsreels were shown. She hated Franklin and Eleanor Roosevelt and, for some similar unknowable reason, Claire Booth Luce. Whenever they appeared on the screen, she would stand up and loudly boo.

She also was a fan of spy stories. From them she got the notion that dangerous men employed by foreign governments were following her. Sometimes, when she was shopping, she would approach a policeman and point out some well-dressed, middle-aged man who she claimed had been following her and demand that he be arrested on the spot.

Usually the policeman would question her for a while and then, would become the target of my mother's fury and sharp tongue by trying to persuade her she had an overactive imagination.

"The police are in league with the spies," she would confide to me afterward.

But sometimes a zealous policeman would confront the bewildered man who was the object of my mother's suspicions. There would follow a series of angry or anguished denials from the victim which would end with the man being released and the policeman attempting to pacify my, by this time, angry mother.

The result would further convince her that the police were part of an international conspiracy.

She divided people between the watched and the watchers, she being both.

She was suspicious, not only of authorities and strangers, but of store owners and proprietors of businesses.

For most of the years when I was growing up we had no telephone. One reason for this was that for many years we couldn't afford one. Another reason was that my mother had a poor memory about who she had called and believed people were breaking into the house to use our phone to call long distance. Her argument with the phone company over the bill would end with her demanding that the telephone be taken out of the house immediately.

Other times she had the telephone taken out because, when she answered the phone, strangers would sometimes insist they had called the wrong number, an excuse my mother never accepted. Those calling had not innocently misdialed a number. They were part of an international plot to force her to divulge the secret behind the Amelia Earhart disappearance.

"I don't know who they are but, they're doing it deliberately," she would say. They're trying to torment me, mean, spiteful people. I don't know what it is they think I know."

She got into the habit of trying to disguise her voice when she answered the phone so the people trying to bedevil her would not get the satisfaction of knowing that they were talking to the right person.

She once asked the telephone company for an unlisted number, but on learning it would mean an extra charge on our telephone bill, she settled for removing the number from the telephone handset, arguing that it would prevent anyone breaking into the house from copying the number off the wheel that dialed the number. Why anyone would break in the house to learn our telephone number when they could look it up in the telephone directory she didn't say and I didn't dare to ask her.

She habitually looked at the dark side of an accomplishment, a situation or a milestone in our turbulent lives. Her purse weighed enough to serve as an anchor for a small boat, a result of her insistence on regularly converting folding money into coins because she feared a change in government at the next election would make paper bills useless.

When I was nearing my graduation from grade school, she warned me not to be surprised to find I had been given a blank diploma. "They hate us in this parish because we live in a little house. Don't think for one minute they're going to let you graduate."

When I was a man and she came to see my wife and I when we were living less than an hour's drive from Niagara Falls, she refused to view the great attraction from the Canadian side for fear she would not be allowed to return to the U.S.

She lived in a cruel world of perpetual darkness. Sunshine was wasted on her.

Chapter 3

The Neighborhood

I was grown up before the arrival of the Service Economy, a term that is like calling crop harvesting a country vacation.

When I was a child, pleasant-voiced women were employed to help people talk long distance person to person on the telephone. Ushers used small flashlights to help movie goers find seats. Gasoline station attendants cleaned windshields and checked the oil and tires. A golf course might have a hundred caddies or more to carry golfer's clubs. Store clerks got the canned goods and cereals you wanted down from the shelves themselves and if you couldn't make it to the grocery, bread wagons and milk trucks and fruit and vegetable wagons several times a week came down the street clanging bells announcing their arrival. Family-owned stores delivered groceries and medicines to the door without charging extra for the service.

Since we often didn't have a car during those years, we took advantage of those delivery services -- but never for long periods of time, for my mother would soon become suspicious of the milk truck driver or the bread delivery man, insisting they were Protestants who were intent on poisoning Catholics, or part of the worldwide conspiracy trying to make her helpless by driving her out of her mind.

She would switch companies or buy the items at the store or wait until a new deliveryman was on our route before going back to the service and then repeating the cycle.

Mr. Stephens, a balding, rotund, middle-aged man who owned Stephens Groceries, for several years cheerfully delivered our orders to our house.

He was forever polite and had a pleasant greeting when he came. The orders were always correctly filled and the prices were fair. Try as she might, my mother could find nothing to complain about. Nor did he do anything to fire her hair-trigger suspicions until a stormy winter night when he slipped on the ice on our back porch, spilling the box of groceries and landing awkwardly on his back, but arising unhurt.

My mother never did business with his store again. She claimed he was looking for ways to sue us out of all our money.

She also stopped getting her prescriptions filled at Schumann's Drug Store after Mr. Schumann gave me a piece of penny candy for walking the six blocks from our house to return a dime we owed him. It was Lent and I given up candy as my Lenten sacrifice.

"I knew I shouldn't have sent you alone," she said. "Damn Jew! He'd do anything to get a Catholic boy to break his Lenten resolution."

My mother's suspicions of wrongdoing extended to most of the neighbors. Although Girard Avenue had little of the crime and violence we have learned to endure today, she had triple locks installed on all the doors and extra locks on all the windows. She carefully locked the doors to the two small bedrooms while we were in the house.

It was a tiny house at the back of a lot about 50 feet wide and 100 feet long. It had started out as a garage, but the original owner, running short on money, had divided the original building into two bedrooms, then dug out a basement for a coal furnace and added a living room and dining room, a kitchen and a bathroom.

If my father or I stepped into the yard for even a few minutes, we were commanded to lock the door behind us. She bought metal cabinets and boxes with sturdy locks in which she would store the cosmetics she peddled for Avon, costume jewelry and -- during World War II -- such scarce items as sugar and pepper.

Despite these precautions, she was convinced that the neighbors were regularly breaking in the house. Whenever she couldn't find something she would blame the loss on someone entering the house at night and taking it.

When it was argued that the item missing was a screwdriver or a spoon or something of little value, while cash was lying on the dresser, she would reply: "They're doing it deliberately to devil me. They're trying to drive me out of my mind."

21

Inevitably with all the locking of doors and windows, some one would be left outside the triple locked empty house without a key. That meant smashing a window to get in.

When that happened it would send my father into a tantrum in which he would curse, pound his fists into the window frame and fling his tools, or anything else at hand, though the broken window before calming down and set about replacing the glass.

I don't know what caused my mother's mania for locking things up as though the house held the only copy of the secret formula for the original Coca Cola. Did it come from some terrible experience that happened in her youth?

She was born in Blue Earth, Minnesota in 1894, the second youngest of five children. Her mother was a fiercely Irish girl who had married Joseph Rollins, of English descent. He had been born in Lowell, Massachusetts in 1857. A few months later, his father, Eliphet, took the family west to Minnesota where he established a farm.

Joseph Rollins spent his childhood on the farm, helping his mother and his nine siblings run it after Eliphet left to travel to the far West.

A portrait taken in a Winnebago City studio around 1895 shows a large, tall man seated wearing sturdy shoes, striped pants, an open coat with narrow lapels, a vest and beneath it a shirt with a high button collar and a cravat. He is balding and has a bearded chin and a tiny mustache. The whole appearance is that of a fairly prosperous man with average looks wearing a grim expression as though sitting for the portrait was an onerous duty, which he was reluctantly, but manfully, fulfilling.

Next to him is a small, serious-looking young woman, her dark hair pinned up over her ears in curls, some of which hang over her forehead. She wears a dark dress, which covers her from her shoes to her high neck collar. Her face is on the pretty side, but it has an unfinished appearance as though it were a portrait in which the artist had not yet painted in cheekbones or lines.

At the time of the photo, Rollins was co-owner and proprietor of the Winnebago City Foundry and Machine Shops. A few years afterward he died and his widow and children moved to the farm of my foster mother's uncle near Dubuque, Iowa. He was a mean and hard man, according to my mother. She often complained of him forbidding her and her brothers and sisters to talk at the table. Eventually, he sent her rebellious oldest brother, Ethan, away to Our Lady of Victory boys' school in Lackawanna, N.Y.

I don't know if my mother would have been a different person had her father lived until she was a young woman. I do know that her widowed mother made certain she was raised in the Catholic faith and taught her an undying hatred of the English, which, considering her mother's choice of husband, is curious.

But no stranger than the fact my mother similarly selected a husband from a nationality she detested.

She called Italians "dirty Dagoes." Italians were only slightly more honest than Jews and their morals were only a little better than those of Negroes. Italians were people who cried and showed affection too easily. They were people compelled to lie and steal and who were lazy and ignorant as well. Definitely people not to be trusted. She made fun of my father's sisters, their husbands and their children and only reluctantly would visit their homes.

I don't know where she got her attitudes about Italians. I don't think she came in contact with many when she was being raised on the farm, although I know little of her early life. She either didn't talk about it much or I didn't listen when I was young.

From what she did say and from all accounts of farm life in the Midwest at the turn of the century, it was a hard life with little money, especially for a family with no father.

Helen Rollins went to a school run by nuns through the eighth grade, then, like the majority of Iowa children at the time, she went to work full time on the farm. A few years later, she and her older sister, Mae, joined the wave of young women who, in the early part of the 20th century, followed the railroad lines leading from farm cities in the Midwest to Chicago where there was a better chance of finding a paying job, a measure of independence and perhaps a mate.

Following the railroad also brought my foster father to Chicago. It was one of the few things his wife and he had in common.

Chapter 4

Fighting

My conviction that I couldn't be the natural son of either of my parents was strengthened in second grade. By that time we had moved from Chicago to Canton, Ohio where my father's parents and his three sisters were living.

Our class was to take First Holy Communion in the Roman Catholic Church. My mother, however, couldn't produce the necessary baptismal certificate to allow me to take the sacrament. She insisted I had been baptized but that all records of my baptism had been destroyed in a church fire.

Not only could I not take my first holy communion unless I could prove I was baptized, I couldn't get into heaven either. At that time the belief in Limbo was widespread in the Roman Catholic Church. I wouldn't go to hell just because I wasn't baptized. I would go to a nice place -- a Holiday Inn of the spiritual world -- where I would be content because I didn't know what I was missing.

But I would be denied the happiness of seeing God in all His glory -- the full Ritz Carleton treatment.

I realized I was in grave peril of being forever condemned to tourist class in the next world.

I think the pastor thought so too, although I don't think he believed my mother's story. I was baptized privately at a side altar of the church with one of the parish aldermen -- the father of a boy in the grade above me -- as my godfather.

--My mother insisted that the ceremony be kept secret -- one of the reasons none of my father's relatives were not asked to be godparents. The other being that they were Italians.

It was too good a story to remain hidden. It wasn't long before some of my schoolmates asked if it was true I was adopted. "No!" I replied insistently. "I'm not adopted."

At the time, I was attending second grade in St. Benedict's Elementary School, a yellow brick structure attached to the church, also of yellow brick in a sort of imitation Spanish style. It was a small school with only four classrooms. That meant that the harried nuns assigned to the school each had to teach two grades, both in the same room.

They would spend half the day instructing one grade, while the pupils in the other grade, in theory, were to quietly study and do homework at their desks. The advantage of this arrangement was that if you were in the lower grade you got a preview of the hard stuff that awaited you when you moved up the following year.

But many of us wasted our study time whispering to one another, passing notes (after we were able to write), drawing pictures (in my case rudimentary sketches of fighter planes that looked like boxing gloves firing machine guns mounted in stubby wings, the bullets represented by a series of penciled dashes. I planned to be a fighter pilot shooting down the Germans and Japs when I broke out of school in a couple of years.)

The boys also, out of boredom, punched and kicked any other nearby male. Some boys might occasionally pull a girls hair, but mostly we left them alone. They were usually obediently studying and were apt to tattle.

I could not sit still in the early grades. I wiggled and kicked and used the fold up seat as a back and butt scratcher. Finally, in desperation, my first and second grade teacher, a young nun, Sister Veronica, tied my legs to the desk each day. Otherwise, she was nice to me. She used to keep me after school and try to explain why I should behave and not disturb the other children. She gave me picture books to take home and, once, a puppet set. Finally, she gave up trying to civilize me and went to China where converting the heathens seemed a much easier task.

Second grade was also the time when many of my schoolmates stopped playing with me. My mother's paranoia convinced her they were beating me up as on my way home from school. My denials only convinced her I was too frightened to admit it.

She would question me until I cowardly gave up the names of the boys who had been with me, still denying that anyone had touched me.

My mother would call the parents of each of the boys who had walked home with me and accuse their sons of savagely beating me up. Too often her accusations   resulted in my classmates being unfairly punished.

But if they couldn't be friends with me, they couldn't avoid fighting with me. There were few days when I didn't have a fight with some other boy during my grade school days. I would fight for trivial reasons or none at all. I would fight during recess. I would fight during lunch hour. (Most of us ate lunch at home.) I would fight after classes ended at 3:30 p.m.

Usually, I lost since I was not a good fighter and didn't seem able to learn from my constant defeats. In addition, I was underweight for my height during my school days and often I would fight several boys at the same time. Sometimes we fought with our fists, sometimes we wrestled, sometimes both. Sometimes, on the way home, instead of fighting, I and the other boys simply threw stones and rocks at each other.

The nuns often kept me in the classroom during recess because of my fighting and rock throwing and other misdeeds. I usually got an A in reading and my other grades weren't bad, but my report card always had written on it two "P"s for poor, the lowest possible mark. They were for handwriting and character.

While I lost most of my fights, I got a reputation I was proud of. It was for never crying no matter how hard or how many times I was hit.

"You can't make him cry. Hit him and see. He won't cry." Boys who had fought with me or seen me defeated would rouse other boys.

Boys were lining up to see if they could make me cry. Boys from other schools took up the challenge. Kids visiting from other states would enter the competition. I was like a celebrated gunfighter every top gun in the West wanted to challenge because killing him would make them famous.

But, while I collected bruises and fat lips like a persistent novice skier on an Olympic downhill, I manfully retained my painfully earned reputation.

I rarely cried at home when I was smacked for some indiscretion, which happened on the average of once a day. When I did cry, it was not because of pain, but because of anger and a feeling of injustice.

Both my parents were strong believers in the adage "Spare the rod and spoil the child." In my case, they thought the need for discipline was particularly acute. They believed children born out-of-wedlock were bad seeds.

Usually, my mother administered the punishment since she was the one most likely to be around. Most often, it was in the form of a few smart slaps in the face, although sometimes she used the broom handle to strike at whatever part of me was handy and once or twice she used a toy whip that I had won at the annual summer church festival.

My sins were many, although I don't recall most of them now. A big one was leaving the yard after they bought the house on Girard Avenue when I was in third grade.

I think she was afraid I would be kidnapped by foreign agents or perhaps by minions of my natural mother, or perhaps it was seen as a measure to curb my inherited willfulness.

Actually, the yard wasn't any bigger than a narrow city lot, which were 50 feet across. It looked bigger because the house was in the back of the lot where most of the neighbors had gardens. Despite my mother's commandment, I disobediently snuck away from the yard from time to time in search of a worthy foe.

My father, as most of the fathers in the parish, worked a rotating swing shift which changed weekly, 3 to 11 p.m.; 11 p.m. to 7 a.m., 7 a.m. to 3 p.m. When I got home from school, he was either at work or sleeping. Mill fathers were not very important in the lives of their sons.

When my father was home, his mood usually depended on whatever words had recently passed between him and my mother. More often than not, they would have been sharp.

They were opposite in nearly every respect. He was a man of volatile, and sometimes violent passions. She was cold and standoffish and was repulsed by any demonstrations of affection. The greater his need, the colder she became.

I remember him raising his fists often, but I don't recall him ever actually striking her. She was the dominant force in the house. We lived by her often puzzling rules. He handed over his paycheck to her every two weeks, as he had given his wages to his mother.

She would give him spending money, but he often complained to me when I was older that she didn't give him enough money to keep him in cigarettes the whole two weeks between paychecks.

He often hit me when he was angry with something I had done, sometimes putting up his fists in a boxer's stance and challenging me to hit him back.

"Come on, come on, hit me back. Come on, hit me! You're yellow! Come on, hit me, so I can really take a swing at you."

I was not fool enough to try to hit him.

There were a few times when his anger and frustrations erupted in an unrestrained tantrum in which he would punch holes in the wall, break down a door and then grab the butcher knife from a drawer in the kitchen and threaten to kill my mother and me and then himself. Once he went into the bathroom where the arsenic for the garden pests was store and emerged with his lips and teeth purple.

"I've just taken enough arsenic to kill me," he said. "If it doesn't kill me, I'm going to cut my throat right here before you." He held the blade of the butcher knife to his throat.

My mother's response was to leave the house with me. We caught a city bus a half block away. (My mother gave up driving after she drove into the trunk of a bootlegger's car in Chicago and smashed the barrel of liquor that was in it.)

"He didn't take enough to kill him," my mother said. "He doesn't have the guts. I think he spit it out. He just wants our sympathy. Well, he's not going to get it." She was right on both counts.

Eventually, his murderous passions would subside and he would be racked with guilt. He sometimes knelt in front of me and asked me to forgive him. I felt neither hate nor anger nor satisfaction. I was embarrassed. I whispered a timid: "I forgive you."

And I did. I believe that -- despite their impulses to inflict pain, their coldness and passions, weaknesses and irrationalities, they loved me -- as much as they were capable of loving anything.

We couldn't afford a doctor, except for the most serious illness, so when I was sick or injured, I was treated with home remedies: a bread and milk poultice around the wound to draw out the poison when I stepped on a rusty nail; crushed onions, lemon juice and sugar, followed by a glass of port wine for the flu.

To ease a cough, my parents relied religiously on Father John's cough medicine, a muddy-looking syrup with gray liquid that swirled around the spoon after it was poured, looking something like water from a clay-bottomed pond that had just been disturbed. It had a sweet, chalky taste. If holy water could chase away devils and vampires, surely medicine concocted by the saintly-looking and wise elderly priest on the bottle could work a miracle in fighting a simple cold.

Once, noticing how thin I was, my mother decided I needed vitamin C. I'm not sure why she picked C out of all the alphabetical vitamins, but I suspect it was something she had heard on the radio, one of those commercial public service messages in the interval between *Ma Perkins* and *Guiding Light*.

However, on learning the price of vitamin C tables at the drug store, she changed her diagnosis. I was getting sufficient amounts of vitamin C, she decided. But I was deficient in vitamin E, which, as luck would have it, was only half the price.

She was also a firm believer in the health benefits of cod liver oil tablets -- little pills in the shape of tiny footballs made of some transparent material that tasted and felt like soft plastic and was filled with a tan, oily liquid.

She gave me random doses of whatever pills and medicines she thought proper to cure current ailments as fever, weight loss or itchy skin. Sometimes they made me sick to my stomach and gave me the runs, but I credit them with saving me from lockjaw, scarlet fever, polio and tuberculosis, all childhood diseases that were relatively common then.

Most of us tested positive for tuberculosis sometime during our school days. It was something you had and got over, like the flu, or you died in Molly Stark, the TB sanitarium, a sprawling complex of buildings in the rolling country side outside Canton. A couple of my classmates died there from it, as did a cousin, a pretty girl, Madeline Cerrani. I suppose there were sanitarium patients who recovered but I never knew any. I figured you went to Molly Stark you were a goner.

Chapter 5

Sour notes

When I was six, my mother felt I should play the violin. I have no idea why, since I had shown no musical talent and we had little money. Nevertheless, she convinced my father to buy me an old instrument hanging in a pawnshop. It had a small crack in its body, two broken strings and a bow with so many horse hairs missing it looked like a device invented to floss elephant's teeth. But when it was examined by the thin, anxious, dark-haired man who would become my instructor it was discovered to be a -- battered old violin that cost twice as much to repair as my father had begrudgingly paid for it.

It was a time when hundreds of thousands of unemployed men would stoop to do anything for a few dollars. Men came to our door offering to sharpen knives. They offered to paint the house, fix broken appliances, do any needed house repairs, weed the garden, all for a couple of dollars, or, at times, only a meal.

I don't know what Mr. Dix, my violin instructor, had done before the Depression. I like to think he had played first violin with the Cleveland Orchestra and lost his job for putting too much rosin on his bowstrings at a time the management was cutting expenses. I like to think that he had fallen in love with a young woman while hitchhiking through Canton on his way to find a job in Cincinnati and so remained in our city.

Whatever wrong he had done, he looked like he needed a meal and his frayed collar and sleeve ends showed that he needed a new shirt. Unfortunately, he was also a serious lover of music.

Pianists only have to hit the correct key to get the right note. No one can play the violin without signing a pact with the devil.

It defies the laws of physics for a human to press his finger on a taut string in exactly the right place two times in a row while holding a hollow wooden box with his chin and, with his other hand, drawing part of a horse's tail across the string. Not only that, but the string on which the tail is being rubbed must be the right one out of four possible choices. If that isn't difficult enough, consider this: the bow must not touch the other strings. Such a movement cannot be done by a human. It requires the aid of supernatural power, whether from the devil, or from God.

Catholic school kids were compelled to ask a lot of God, mostly through the Virgin Mother and enough saints to triple the population density of California, a place that is not their natural habitat. The nuns told us of angels who came down from heaven and helped boys and girls who prayed for help with their homework -- some even did some of the work for them. I prayed for help a lot. Why study or practice when you can get an angel to do it for you?

I was too scared of authority to pray to God directly to help me find E flat, or to send down one of His angels who could do it. You didn't want to upset someone who could send you directly to hell with trivial matters. I prayed to the fourteen saints or so who had the reputation of being the top agents, the ones who could bypass all the secretaries and personal assistants and get though to God at his private, unlisted number.

 Not even St. Jude, the patron of the impossible, could help. What came out of my violin sounded like a cat with its tail caught under a rocker.

It's hard to believe that Mr. Dix had so many pupils he could afford to lose one. After six weeks of lessons, he still wore frayed shirts and looked like he was on a two week fast. But starvation was preferable to listening to me make the scraping sounds of a rusty hinge. A cow rubbing against a barbed wire fence made more melody.

He told my parents the task was hopeless and was never seen again.

But my mother didn't give up. When I was in sixth grade she bought a small marimba with her Avon money and brought it in the house saying I was to learn to play it.

"We let you choose the violin. Now I'm going to choose what you're going to play."

It was useless to protest that I didn't choose the violin. It was entirely their idea, but they were convinced that my dearest wish when I was six was to become a great violinist.

I had never seen a marimba, which is like a xylophone with long tubes hanging down from it. The ones they use mostly in orchestras that play Latin American music have tubes of polished metal. Mine had cardboard tubes like the ones inside rolls of paper towels and toilet paper, except they were painted silver and had a metal cap on one end.

She choose the marimba for me because the man in the apartment next to us in Chicago had played the instrument at the World's Fair and she had been fascinated watching him hold several mallets in each hand and pound out music.

I never got to the several mallets in each hand phase. But at least when I hit a wooden bar that had "C-" engraved on it, I got "C-."

Chapter 6

Strikes and Riots

One of the events that made a lasting impression was the strike at Republic Steel by workers seeking union recognition, which occurred when I was in second grade.

My father had willingly been a member of the American Federation of Labor when he was a boilermaker. But John L. Lewis' upstart C.I.O. (Committee, later Congress, of Industrial Organizations) was considered more radical, more revolutionary. My mother was among those insisting that the "C" in CIO stood for communist.

In Canton, as in East Chicago and other cities in the seven states Republic Steel had plants, strikers and striker-breakers and platoons of company and municipal police forces fought bloody battles at plant gates and on the streets.

The top management of Republic Steel was determined it would not be unionized. Tom Girder, who headed the company, announced that if every employee signed a union card he would not recognize the union. "I will shut the factories first," he said.

And Republic was well prepared and willing to resist with force. It had a police force of nearly 400 men armed with pistols, rifles and even machine guns. In 1936 it was the nation's largest purchaser of tear gas.

Even before the strike began, Republic fired thousands of workers at its plants in Canton and nearby Massillon in an attempt to scare the rest into rejecting the union.

The most tragic violence in the strike occurred in East Chicago when police fired into the ranks of workers and their families marching toward the steel plant gates, killing 10 and injuring 30 more. Other strikers and their wives were badly beaten.

In all, 18 union men were killed during the strike, three of them in Massillon, just outside of Canton. Republic's chief of the Canton-

Massillon region was shot and wounded. A foreman was wounded in both hands and both legs.

Strikers and strikebreakers both believed they were fighting to feed their families and therefore fought with fury and desperation. Strikebreakers were beaten at the plant gates; they were beaten on their way home from work. Sometimes they were attacked in their homes.

My father was among the strikebreakers. He traveled to and from work each day with a homemade short hose filled with a solid piece of lead pipe to which a leather strap was attached. I never heard that he was attacked himself. He had already earned a reputation for flinging wrenches, lunch boxes and every loose item of metal from his crane when he was angry. So perhaps his reputation for fighting and of having quick, destructive moods was a deterrent.

However, one of his friends, a fellow strikebreaker, was badly beaten on the way to visit him at our house.

I used to watch, with my mother, as my father and other striker-breakers left the mill. Armed National Guardsmen lined the roads leading from the plant for three or four miles and light, single-engine National Guard observer planes flew overhead.

At that time we lived across from a gasoline station and there were usually National Guard trucks refueling there. If I disobeyed my mother and wandered over, often the Guardsmen would buy me a nickel candy bar or coke.

Despite the recurring presence of military trucks across from the house we were renting, threats against my father grew so frequent that, at one period in the strike, he left for a couple of weeks to live with his brother Harry in Willard, Ohio about 80 miles away, while my mother and I remained in Canton.

The striking workers and their families were being fed at union soup kitchens and when the kitchens ran out of food and there were no union dues to buy more, the strike ended with the company victorious.

Five years later, as the country began to arm to fight its World War II enemies, under pressure from the National Labor Relations Board, Republic recognized the union.

My father became a union steward and sometimes took me to union meetings.

I felt no fear watching the men leave the Republic Steel plant during the 1937 strike. Fear was part of the experience much later as I was a reporter covering the violent and destructive riot in Buffalo's black neighborhoods in the wake of the assassination of Martin Luther King in April 1968.

That had not been an easy story to cover. The first reporters ordered to go to the scene to report on what was happening refused. I felt it was part of the job and I wanted to witness the scene. I volunteered.

A photographer and I arrive at the Cold Spring police precinct where authorities had set up headquarters. A Buffalo police captain looks at us and shakes a finger.

"I'm warning you not to go into the area of the rioting. We can't protect you if you get in trouble."

Ignoring the police warning, we team up with a couple of television reporters-photographers who are driving an unmarked, rented car. We go into the heart of the riot area, driving down the center of Jefferson Avenue, the main business section of Buffalo's black area, driving through red lights, going down the middle of the street, stopping briefly to watch the looting, taking quick pictures, then fleeing in the car at high speed when knots of rioters began to cast angry glances at us.

It is scary. It is exhilarating -- like sex for the first time. The heart pumps faster, breath comes shorter and quicker. Adrenaline flows.

"The sounds of civil disorder are the tinkle of broken glass, the muffled crackle of distant shooting, the shouted obscenities directed at policemen, and the hysterical laughter of women," I write in the lead of my story.

"The sights are less dramatic: A Negro man being hustled into a police car, the belligerent faces in a knot of young people, the glitter of broken glass on sidewalks, the fog-like smoke of tear gas, and the orange glow of a dying fire."

Most of those doing the rioting had never met Martin Luther King Jr. I had and was sure he wouldn't have approved.

I interviewed the young black leader in New Haven when he came to speak with the students at Yale in 1959.

"We must never become bitter, nor should we succumb to the temptation of using violence." He talked with convincing earnestness and eloquence and wisdom. "For if violence happens our chief legacy to the future will be an endless reign of meaningless chaos."

We sat in one of the rooms in the master's house in Pierson College, where he was an overnight guest. King sat in a leather-upholstered chair decorated with brass tacks. He wore a dark suit, red tie and white shirt with large gold cuff links.

What impressed me most was his understanding of human nature. When, under his leadership, peaceful disobedience and sit-ins won blacks the right to sit in the front of the bus in Montgomery, Alabama, "I told the people now that you've won, don't rub it in their faces. Don't make a big issue of sitting in the front of the bus. If there's an empty seat in the back, take it. We have to all live together when the battle is over. The Negro cannot seek to defeat or humiliate his opponents, because that will continue the battle."

Prejudice against blacks was part of life in the heavily Catholic working class neighborhood of mixed nationalities in which I was raised. The Catholics were largely descendants of German and Polish immigrants. The Protestants were mostly Anglo-Saxon. The parish also encompassed the Spanish neighborhood on its north side, close to the steel mills where most of the men in the parish worked.

There was a scattering of Italians, but most of them attended St. Anthony's parish further west. There were also a few Irish families.

There were no black children in St. Benedict's grade school and only a few Hispanics. But the nuns preached about the evils of racial discrimination. It was abhorrent to them and a very grave sin that could send you to everlasting hell fire.

It was a message I brought home where my father's prejudices against blacks were far stronger than my mother's railings against "dirty Italians."

He told approvingly of signs he had seen in small Southern cities warning "Nigger don't let the sun go down on your head here." He praised bartenders who smashed glasses from which Negroes had drunk.

His prejudices were not much different from those of the majority of the men he worked with at the steel plant or from those of his relatives. His brother-in-law stopped listening to broadcasts of Cleveland Indian games years later after blacks were allowed on the team.

Racial discrimination, while not enforced by law as it was in the South, was approved in our Ohio society, even by Catholics who went to mass every Sunday, despite the efforts by the idealistic nuns.

When I was 12, I took swimming lessons sponsored by the American Red Cross in the Knights of Columbus pool. Virtually all the boys were Catholic and after we completed the lessons, the K of C club manager encouraged us to join the Squires, a boys club sponsored by the Knights.

Noting that a Negro boy had been taking lesson with us, he promised, "Don't worry. He's not going to be allowed to join."

No one objected. It was the way things were done, and we accepted it.

I was surprised when I began a job as a movie usher at a second run theater next to a black neighborhood to be instructed to seat Negroes in the balcony or at the sides -- unless they objected. At home, I spoke up against my father's prejudices.

"If you're a nigger lover, you should go live with them," was his stock, angry response.

Prejudice is not based on reason. It cannot be changed by argument. I was too young to know that.

The military today is fully integrated at all levels, but when I was in the army in the late 1940s and very early '50s, racial prejudice was very strong. I recall a class in military courtesy in which the sergeant reluctantly told us we were to salute all officers, even if they were black.

"I know how you feel. I feel that way myself. I have to steel myself to do it when I run into a black officer. But you're saluting the bar on his shoulder, not the man."

There were all black regiments and companies, but at the company level and below the races were kept separate.

At Fort Lewis in the state of Washington when I was there, a lake on the property had six separate beaches. One for white enlisted men, one for black enlisted men, one for white non commissioned officers, one for black NCOs, one for black officers and one for white.

My mother was not as crude as my father in expressing her strong prejudices against blacks, but in her frequent fights with the neighbors she would threaten to get even by selling our house to Negroes. Ironically, the house is now occupied by a black family in a black neighborhood in a heavily black parish.

Chapter 7

Funerals

Undertakers were the politest people I knew when I was small. I remember clearly them setting up folding chairs in the cramped living rooms of the homes of my father's dead relatives and I remember how soft spoken and polite they were.

Most of the people in our neighborhood were not soft spoken. The men, most of them, worked in the steel mills where men did not talk with soft voices and they never got the knack of speaking in library tones. Their women laughed loudly and screeched to be heard over the shrill voices of half a dozen quarreling, laughing children. All family conversations were conducted at full volume.

But undertakers talked as though they were always in church and they used go give out nickels to kids who were quiet.

I don't know why, but it seems that all the funerals I went to in my childhood occurred in the summer. I remember how hot it used to get sitting quietly for long periods of time in one crowded room. I wished I could go outside to play or at least read a book. Usually I sat as quietly as I could and kicked the back legs of my chair and watched the blades of the big fan go around. I pretended the fan was the motor of an airplane flying across the Atlantic in a violent storm, the plane tossed and shaken by the strong wind, losing attitude, one motor gone, threatening to plunge into the icy sea. I looked anxiously at the whirling blades.

There was pink netting over the casket of some of my aunts but when my grandfather, a small man with a big white mustache, died there was no netting and I amused myself by watching the flies land on his forehead and run around his face.

All the dead people I ever saw when I was little were in caskets, with the exception of one aunt who was lying in a messed-up bed, heavy pink blankets twisted around her, with her eyes half open when I

40

saw her. That was because my uncle said she wasn't dead and fought the undertakers called by one of her sons to take her away.

But all the rest were laid out in elegant caskets of bronze lined with soft, clean fabric that looked more comfortable and certainly was more expensive than the beds in which they had slept and made love.

Among my father's family, the love shown the dead by the surviving members of the family was judged rigidly by the cost of the casket, the numbers and sizes of the baskets of flowers and the size and quality of the headstones.

A cutting remark about ungratefulness could be expected if a wife, husband, son, daughter bought a headstone that didn't meet family standards.

Funerals were the only time that all the members of my father's family got together. Young men were flown from overseas where they had been fighting the Germans or the Japs. Relatives whose names I had heard only once or twice came from Detroit, from Pittsburgh, from New Orleans.

At the wake of one of my aunts, the governor let her eldest son out of the state penitentiary in Columbus to view the body and attend the funeral mass. He came unobtrusively accompanied by a prison guard in plain clothes.

That was an exception, even for our family. Most of my father's relatives were hardworking, law-abiding men and woman. Violent and passionate and quarrelsome at funerals and weddings maybe, but not guilty of major violent crime.

I did have a cousin who was said by some of the relatives to be a made member of the mafia, but I didn't see him much.

To have someone in mafia was not a source of pride among my father's relatives. It was gossiped in tones of disapproval.

On the day of the funeral of one of my father's family, just before the casket was closed, everyone present would line up and kiss the forehead of the dead person. I recall how cold and hard it was, like a rock, and the smell of face powder when you bent over. My grandfather was the first dead person I ever kissed and I didn't think it was right to put so much powder on him, since he never used it when he was alive.

My father's relatives did not mourn their dead quietly. As the casket was being carried out of the house, the older women would begin to wail and scream and try to throw themselves on top of it. They would moan and tear their hair and then collapse in a fit-like faint.

That's when the quarrels would begin. Men and women would divide into sides. One side would attempt to elevate the collapsed mourner's feet contending the blood should rush to the head. The other side, arguing that the blood should flow away from the skull, would put the victim's large, black pattern leather purse under her head.

"The feet! The feet!" Uncle Charlie would say, grabbing the woman's ankles and lifting them in the air.

"No, the head!" would insist cousin Angelo, lifting the woman's shoulders until, as a result of their actions, her body was in the shape of an open safety pin.

While this struggle was going on between the good Samaritans, Aunt Mary would douse the unconscious mourner with holy water from a small bottle she carried in her large purse.

At this point, the undertaker would step in and, in his quiet, dignified, official voice, restore order and decorum. As I said, they were the politest people I knew.

Mostly at the family wakes, I brought a book to read. As I grew older and had more time by myself than most boys my age, I turned to reading as an escape. It was an activity I learned from my mother. She loved reading, particularly detective stories and mysteries. She collected old readers from the time she went to school, that I read many times over. I found Longfellow and Emerson far more exciting than Dick and Jane.

For many years we couldn't afford delivery of the newspaper and she tried to forbid me from deciphering Shakespeare on the grounds he was anti-Catholic and immoral, but she paid for a subscription to *The Catholic Boy* that featured the chase adventures of Biff O'Malley from Loyola, the Irish-American seventh son of a seventh son. And on my birthday and at Christmas I received presents of books. I developed a special fondness for stories and poems with sad endings. *The Song of*

Rolland in my fourth grade reader, with its tragic death of the hero, was my favorite among all the stories I read in the lower grades.

Along with most other kids, I read comic books. Usually I read them at the Ralph's home, when I was allowed to go there. I didn't read them at home or at school because the nuns didn't approve of them and my mother forbade me to read them on the grounds the vivid colors injured a child's eyes. In addition, she didn't approve of the scantly clothed women on the pages. As a whole, she thought they were immoral, in the same category as Shakespeare.

Chapter 8

The Prize

On Sunday mornings on Girard Avenue in those days of my youth, the Catholics walked to church in groups of three or four down the middle of the asphalt-paved street shaded by maple trees. The houses on each side were largely wood framed, two-story structures with partly enclosed front porches on which there was a swing. There were many vacant lots and in the spring some of the neighbors would pay a farmer to come with his horse and plow one or more of the lots for planting. We rented the vacant lot to the north of us and my father, and later I, in spring spaded the rich, rock-free soil ourselves.

The march of the Catholics was repeated on Sunday evenings for benediction and on Thursday nights for Holy Hour. Mr. Nobis, who lived five houses away, drove his Pontiac to benediction with his three sons. Sometimes I rode with them and after the evening service he bought us all ice cream cones. Then he drove to a hill overlooking the coke mills at Republic Steel and we watched the furnaces being opened and the red hot coke, like burning baseballs, pour into waiting railroad cars. It was as good as fireworks, watching bright waterfalls of fire and sparks.

I attended church a lot when I was a boy. The school day began at 7 a.m. when we went to mass before the beginning of classes. If you think that influenced us to be quiet and devout during the service and more obedient pupils in class afterward, you have forgotten that boys are essentially impulsive and untamed wild beasts.

A favorite entertainment during mass was to reach over the pew when we were kneeling and slide the schoolbooks of the boy in front of us to the other end of the pew, where a kneeler at the other end would slide them back. This continued all through communion.

A more difficult pastime was to step on the leg or ankle of the kneeling boy or girl in front of you. It was difficult because it required a considerable amount of bodily contortion. You had to sit up straight on one knee while raising the other leg over the kneeler and then bear down with all the weight you could muster on the leg or ankle in front of you.

It required agility and a good balance because the act had to be done with as little visible motion as possible so as to not alert the nun kneeling three or four rows in back. You knew that if she spotted you she was likely to swoop down on and whack you hard on the back of the head.

A few boys used the crucifix on their rosary to carve their initials or a message on the back of the seat in front of them. But that was considered sacrilegious and you would immediately go to hell if you were struck and killed by a car that day on the way home before you could go to confession or make an act of perfect contrition.

Once in the classroom, the school day begins with a prayer, and a droning recitation of the Pledge of Allegiance to America. We recite the Angelus at lunchtime and, during Lent, end the school day by attending the doleful Stations of the Cross.

Saturdays was the only day when I didn't go to mass. That lasted until my mother became ill when I was in the third grade. She made me promise God that if she recovered, I would go to mass every day, even on Saturdays. She said she would make the promise herself, but it would be better if I made it, since God listened to the prayers of little children.

Ralph, and many of the other boys, spent even longer hours than I in church because they were altar boys who had the privilege of assisting the priest at mass. I was envious. I saw myself in a cassock and surplice rattling off Latin prayers with the devout assurance of Spencer Tracy in *Boys Town* and lighting the tall candles with a calm, artistic flourish that dazzled adults attending the mass. In my imagination, the masses at which I was an altar boy overflowed with parishioners who went to extraordinary lengths for the excitement of watching me carry the Gospel from one side of the altar to the other.

I fancied men switching their work schedules to see St. Benedict's star altar boy in live action, women arising earlier than usual to go to weekday masses at which I was assigned. Even non-Catholics would crowd the pews to watch the wonder altar boy. I pictured some going to the priest afterward and asking to be converted to the Catholic faith. Alas, in fourth grade when volunteers were requested for the task, I was rejected by my teacher. No boy whose character was consistently described as poor could become an altar boy.

I used to daydream a lot when I was in school. I saw myself carrying the ball for Notre Dame on the opening kickoff of the football season, scoring touchdown after touchdown.

Most of the nuns complained to my parents of my day dreaming in class.

"If he would pay more attention to his studies and behave better, he could be at the top of his class." I think teachers in every generation since education became compulsory have said that to all parents of boys and girls who were in the bottom three-fourths of their class.

But Sister Ulrich, who I had in fifth and sixth grade, saw something more sinister in my daydreams. She told the class I was thinking immoral thoughts.

Billy Cooke, a tough Irish kid from a poor family with a dozen children who used to regularly kick my butt on the playground bravely came to my defense.

"Maybe he's just thinking of hitting a ball over the fence," he suggested to sister.

Sister Ulrich shook her head. "I can tell from his eyes what he's thinking," she said.

The girls all shook their combed heads and looked at me with sour expressions of distaste. I sat quietly feeling guilty of some great sin that was going to send me to hell, unless I became a martyr when the great persecution of Catholics in the U.S. erupted as sister often predicted. I felt blood rushing to my face and I knew it was being taken as an admission of my sexual crimes.

As punishment for my sins against the sixth commandment, Sister Ulrich forbade my classmates to speak to me. I was not to be spoken to or played with during recess, during class breaks, lunch hour or on the way home from school.

For the next couple of weeks, my classmates would look at me guiltily and pass me by without speaking or looking at me.

Finally, one day Bill Cooke, always the first to be defiant, said a few words to me during recess and one by one most of the other boys gradually began talking to me. But Sister Ulrich never removed her ban.

***

The life of most nuns at that time was sheltered. They spent their days in the classroom, their nights in the convent and their weekends and odd hours at prayer without much contact with laymen or laywomen except through parental conferences about the boys and girls in their charge.

They never went to a movie, or played Bingo in the parish hall or attended the Sunday church chicken dinners. Nor, were they often seen in stores. They didn't drive cars and had very little contact with non-Catholics. They hid their hair behind concealing wimples and wore heavy, loose fitting habits intended to hide anything remotely resembling feminine allure. They led sexless lives and were paid virtually nothing for a great deal of challenging work and responsibility.

It's small wonder that they were often tense and sharp with us and lost patience. Still, many of them were kindly and had a sense of humor. They ran the spectrum from those unsuited by training or temperament to be teachers of young children to those who were patient, knowledgeable and remarkably able instructors.

Above all, they were dedicated to God and to giving us a basic and moral education. But Sister Ulrich was an extreme example of the minority who were odd, wrongly judgmental and temperamentally unsuited to be teachers. But then, as a father and the husband of a schoolteacher as well as a former education reporter, I have come across a few public school teachers with the same traits.

Chapter 9

Father Gregory

The pastor during most of my school days was an authoritative Benedictine monk of Irish descent, Father Gregory, who patrolled the parish on Sundays looking for male parishioners who were dishonoring the Sabbath by doing physical labor.

If a man was doing non-emergency repair work on his house or spading his garden, Father Gregory would call him to his car out of earshot of the children and remind him it was the Lord's day and he was setting a poor example.

The man would sheepishly go back to the house or garden and begin picking up his tools, telling his children they would continue the work in a day or so.

It was God's intention, however, that women be allowed to do the necessary cleaning and cooking.

In those days, the pastor ruled the parish in working class Catholic neighborhoods. He had far more education than most of the men in the parish. He was often articulate and opinionated and he had been called by God to lead us to a far better place.

Father Gregory was all of that in spades. He was our political advisor, marriage counselor, social worker, grief counselor, guidance counselor, financial advisor, matchmaker, dispute arbitrator, peacemaker and psychologist. A determined, forceful man and a natural leader, he performed all of those tasks with authority and skill. In the midst of the Great Depression, he was able to see to it that every parish child who wanted to attend St. Benedict's could do so. No tuition was charged --and he paid off the parish debt.

He did it largely by convincing every man and woman that it was their church and parish. He got money from those who had it. He got work from the vast majority who didn't.

If the church roof had to be fixed, the men in the parish did it. If painting was required, the men did it.

When the church bell fell down and had to be replaced, he bought a used bell weighing half a ton and the men in the parish did the dangerous, unfamiliar work of installing it high in the bell tower, while he stood on the ground and prayed that there would be no injuries.

If an able-bodied man came to the rectory to ask that his child be baptized, or that a marriage be performed, he was likely to be convinced that his help was needed at the annual church festival or it was necessary for him to help spread stones and ashes on the wet school playground the following week.

If the school and church needed to be cleaned, the women did it. Altar cloths or vestments needed to be repaired or laundered, the women did it.

The women did the cooking and serving at Sunday benefit chicken dinners. They provided the desserts and made the coffee at benefit card parties and Bingo games, while the men set up the tables and chairs and sold the cards and the older children helped clean up afterward.

Our social life revolved around the parish. Dinners and card games and Bingo, Holy Name meetings and shuffleboard afterward. Summer picnics and softball -- the married men against the single men. Horseshoes.

Theater going meant going to the church hall to attend a light comedy or a religious play staged by the parish drama group. We had stars -- just like the movies!

There were play competitions among the various parishes and awards given for best actor, best actress, best director, best production.

When we reached high school we went to dances and hayrides and parties sponsored by the parish Catholic Youth Organization.

And every summer we looked forward to the weeklong parish festival with its games of chance and skill, food, beer and pop.

Memories. The fishpond and its guaranteed prize of a cheap toy. Throw a ball and try to knock the quarter off the pin. Hard kernels of yellow corn used to mark the called numbers on Bingo cards.

When I was in grade school, I ran errands for the men in the parish pounding together the various booths on the school playground. I religiously picked up the loose nails they dropped. All my high school years I was assigned to the balloon booth under my father, who was in charge. I blew up balloons and hawked darts. "Three for a quarter. Only three for a quarter. Get your darts here. Come on! Bust a balloon!"

In those years of the 1930s and '40s, we Catholics in the American Midwest were still not fully accepted as people believing in the same values as our fellow citizens. We stood apart. We had our own different beliefs on the basic things as gambling, drinking and sex. Our religious leaders prayed in an exotic, mysterious language no one else in the world knew or understood. We had our own schools and who outside of staunch Catholics knew what unpatriotic things were taught in them?

Our heroes included Washington and Lincoln, Jefferson and Franklin, but not Tom Paine or Carnegie or Rockefeller or Ford or the American volunteers fighting Franco.

Our special heroes were Knute Rockne, George Gipp, St. Patrick, St. Francis and the Virgin Mary.

And we, at an early age, were given strict mandates to be separate from other religions. Fellowship was not a word Catholics used much and certainly never fellowship with Protestants.

We were forbidden to enter churches or temples or synagogues of other faiths, except for a wedding of a close friend, but we were not to participate in the ceremony.

Priests and ministers today sometimes jointly officiate at 'mixed marriages,' but then a Catholic could marry a Protestant only with great difficulty and it had to be in the rectory, not in the church.

When we were in eighth grade and most of us were preparing to go on to public high school, Father Gregory summoned the class to church and reminded us we were forbidden to join the YMCA or the YWCA or the Hi-Y.

"That C doesn't stand for Catholic. Those organizations are associated with Protestant churches."

Protestants could get to heaven, since they were baptized, but they didn't belong to the only church in the whole universe founded by Christ himself.

The dreaded Protestants. Our chief contact with the public school kids came on All Saints Day, the feast of the Immaculate Conception of the Virgin Mary and St. Gregory's day -- the name day of the pastor.

On those days, gangs of St. Benedict's boys would parade past the nearby public school shouting and laughing and displaying our unrestrained freedom before the envious public kids imprisoned inside.

On Columbus and Armistice Days and other occasions when we were condemned to attend classes while the public school pupils frolicked, the boys from Belden Street School would make a quick invasion of the St. Benedict's school yard loudly demonstrating their liberty.

So, for most of the St. Benedict's graduates, public high school would be the first prolonged contact with Protestants their own age. I think Father Gregory was afraid that it could lead to 'mixed marriages' and eating meat on Fridays.

A few years later, after graduating from Central Catholic High School, I traitorously joined the Canton Hikers Club, mostly Protestant young men and women who rendezvoused Sunday afternoons at the steps of the local YMCA before driving out in the countryside to begin the hike. Each time I arrived at the steps I feared the wrath of Father Gregory should he happen to wander downtown during one of his patrols of the parish.

Even before our final year in eighth grade, the nuns would start talking to us about vocations. I already knew mine. I was going to be a fighter pilot like the John Wayne in *The Flying Tigers.* I would be flying P40s over in China and helping Chiang Kai-shek defeat the evil Japs. It wouldn't be the highest vocation, but it was good enough for me.

The highest vocation was the priesthood. Priests were the representatives on earth of Christ Himself. Only their fingers could touch a consecrated host. Only they could bring Christ down from heaven every morning.

They loved God and his church and the people in it and had strong characters able to resist sins of the flesh.

Most priests were not rich in material goods, but they had something more important -- spiritual wealth awaiting them in heaven. And, according to the sisters, they were very happy, even though they worked long hours and didn't have wives.

Nuns were happy too, even though they were not as high on the religious pecking order as priests. They didn't represent Christ the way a priest did, since Christ was a man. That was not a problem. They strove to follow the example of the Virgin Mary, who was the Mother of God and the one we should pray to if we really wanted to get something done.

It's not by coincidence that the colors of virtually every Catholic school in the U.S., even macho schools like Notre Dame, are blue and white, Our Lady's colors.

Marriage was also a satisfactory state of life, but not quite as high as being a priest or a nun. It was for the weaker men and women more concerned with physical pleasures than with their spiritual life, the kind of people who left places like New York and Ohio to retire in Florida.

I thought about the priesthood, but I knew that someone who consistently got "P" for character would succumb to the pleasures of the flesh, whatever they were. Besides, church law didn't admit bastards to the priesthood.

We thought of the 1930s and early "40s as "The Modern Age." People drove cars on paved streets. We had electric appliances. Although most people took the train or the bus to travel distances of more than 100 miles, a few brave ones tried airplanes. We talked on telephones. We listened to the radio. *Fibber McGee and Molly, The Lux Hour,' Mr. District Attorney*, Lionel Barrymore and Agnes Moorehead in *Mayor of the Town, I Love a Mystery*, Jack Benny, Charlie McCarthy and Fred Allen.

Still, we lived among a couple of the last fading visages of the 19th century. A few farmers still used horses to plow small lots. A horse pulled the Sterling Bread wagon that came past the house. Twice a week in the late spring and summer the ice truck went by, dripping water from its tailgate. People along the street showed they wanted to buy ice and the pound size block needed by putting a card in a front window with black numbers written large: 25, 50, 75, 100.

Seeing a sign, the driver, a man with the build of a Sumo wrestler and wearing a soaked blue shirt and dark pants, would stop the truck, waddle to its rear and pull down the tail gate. The ice was stacked tightly in 100-pound blocks scored into four parts, each quarter representing 25 pounds — at least that was what the blocks weighted when the truck left the plant, before as much as 10 percent of their mass had dissolved and dripped onto the hot pavements over which the truck had passed and was now rapidly turning into water vapor.

The driver reached into the back of the truck with his large, curved tongs and pulled one of the 100 pound blocks toward him. For any size less than 100 pounds, he used an ice pick to break off the proper size, pounding the pick into the blue-white ice, sending pieces of icy shrapnel flying around him.

That job completed, he picked up the block of ice with a pair of large curved tongs and slung it onto his shoulder, resting it on a wide leather pad he wore to keep the ice's cold from piercing his skin. Then sweating and breathing heavily he carried the block into the house.

As soon as he was gone from sight, kids from the neighborhood, myself among them, rushed the truck, climbed onto the tail gate, reaching our hands into the damp truck in violation of the sign posted on its side, in violation of our parent's repeated warnings, scooped up the pieces of ice, then ran and sucked and bit the hard, clear chunks dripping water and tasting faintly of wet wood.

My parents didn't get a refrigerator until the ice truck stopped coming in the early '50s. My mother contended refrigerators were too noisy.

Chapter 10

Children's Games

As I got older, I was allowed beyond the limits of the yard more frequently and played more often with other children. Our games and pastimes were exclusively children's affairs, not midget league versions of sports played by professional athletes. They were played without adult supervision, without adult rules or instruction -- except to be home when the streetlights were turned on.

They were played on the sidewalk or in the street or in vacant lots. They were played without coaches or uniforms or adult spectators or the proper equipment or hope of a future college scholarship or of seeing our names in the paper.

Sometimes we used a rolled-up stocking cap as a football, the only equipment we needed. We used rocks or books or trees for bases when we played softball and, when we needed players, that was most of the time, we allowed girls to play on both sides, even though they sometimes didn't seem to appreciate our tolerance and would refuse to pointlessly try to beat out an easy grounder.

(Another annoyance with girls who played with us during that time was that they seldom held their hands up high in the air properly when they were taken prisoner in a game of cops and robbers. They would hold them part way up, like someone reluctant to ask a question. But they refused to be submissive when threatened by our toy guns.)

Some games, like jumping rope, or jacks or hopscotch -- the lines drawn with chalk in crooked lines on the sidewalk—were exclusively girls' games.

Marbles was mostly a boys' game, played only in the spring. Each of us had our favorite shooter: a "sticker," named in the misguided belief it had a special quality of sticking inside a lopsided ring drawn with a stick on the bare ground. The object was to use your shooter to hit a marble and make it fly outside the ring. If your shooter stayed inside the circle, you got to shoot at one of the remaining marbles.

Sometimes on my way home from school, I gave up rock throwing to play "chasees," a game in which the marble was shot ahead of you and it was then your opponents goal to capture it by hitting it. I was not a good marble shooter. Each year I lost all my marbles by Easter time.

Most boys carried pocketknives that were used to whittle and to play "baseball," done by flipping the knife on the ground with two open blades at right angles to each other. Short blade in the ground "home run;" long blade in the ground "double;" and handle end and long blade in contact with the ground a "single."

Our contests were played for fun, not praise or trophies. And when we grew old enough to discover girls were no longer nuisances, we stopped playing them. And now they are gone, or almost gone. Gone like the Hula Hoop, the skateboard and Davy Crockett hats.

When I was 14 my father thought I should have a rifle—one of the few times I remember him overriding my mother's wishes. He brought home a used .22 caliber, single-shot, bolt action Springfield. A man who worked with my father was selling it. I pay ten dollars out of coins I had earned over several summers for cutting the lawn and by picking wild blackberries and selling them door to door for a quarter a quart.

He didn't own a gun himself, or hunt, and up until now we had never kept a firearm in the house, not even during the violent 1937 steel strike. I don't know his reasons for bringing the weapon home to me. There were no high school rifle teams in the area. It was too small to be used for large game, and in any case, there are no deer or bear in the county at that time.

We had never seen a wild woodchuck or a possum, or a fox and while there were plenty of rabbits, I doubt that even John Wayne could hit one of them with an unstaged rifle shot.

Whatever his reason, I, like most teenage boys, am thrilled to own a gun. It triggers dreams of defending the house against burglars. Or, I am a sniper hiding prone in the woods by the willow-lined creek where we caught frogs and killing German invaders.

The realization that he can kill easily from a distance can give an immature boy an unaccustomed feeling of power. Not that I tried to kill anyone. But I could have easily done it accidentally, for I was dangerously careless and irresponsible. I make it a point to shoot out the light in front of the house of the police captain who heads the youth department. Coming home with the street darkened, my father sometimes complains to me, "I hope the police catch those kids using rocks to break the streetlights. They should be taught a good lesson."

My practice with the .22 stands me in good stead in the army, where I earn medals for being an expert with the rifle and carbine.

"I knew it was a good thing for me to get him a rifle," my father says to my mother.

My mother's excessive protectiveness extends to haircuts. Even when I am an embarrassed teenager, she insists on going with me to the barbershop, where she is the only woman present. She supervises the cutting of my hair, insisting that the barber cut my hair entirely by hand. Electric clippers, she contends, make the hair grow faster.

So it's surprising that she allows me to take long hikes carrying my rifle. Nor does she forbid me to go into dangerous places like an abandoned tunneled mine Ralph Nobis and I discover on a hike in the barren and ugly strip mines that begin almost at the city limit in southeast Canton.

The roof of the mine had collapsed to the extent we have to crawl into the entrance, but we make sure it is safe before going in. We have seen enough adventure movies to know enough to fire a .22 caliber rifle into the entrance. We believe that, if the mine is ready to collapse, the sound of the shot will start a cave in.

When we don't hear anything fall after the shot, we enter. Water is on the floor and there are tracks of animals, which use it as a den. Some of the timbers have cracked and are rotted. It is a neat place and we go there often.

When I tell my mother about it, she advises me against going back. However, she continues, she won't forbid me because if she did and the mine collapses while we are inside, it would mean that I had committed a serious sin of disobedience and I might not have enough time to make a perfect act of contrition before I die and, as a result, I will spend a long time in Purgatory or even go to eternal hell. Her reasoning sounds just fine to me.

Chapter 11

Sex in a Catholic High School

I have met adults who claim to have fond memories of high school. They were the ones who excelled in team sports or who were able to communicate with the opposite sex.

The problem with high school is that most of us undergo it during adolescence. For us mediocre sinners, there is no need for Purgatory. Adolescence is enough suffering for anyone.

You who have survived teen-age and sleep-ins and proms and your first passionate, lingering kiss know what I mean. It's a period when we grow hair in new places. We don't know who we are and we try to hide our personality by merging our identity with others our own age. We have only vague thoughts about what we want to become as adults, in the unlikely event we survive the perilous teenage years.

My ambition was to get out of high school. World War II would end while we were still in school, ending the need for fighter pilots. It closed off an excuse to leave home that would be acceptable to my foster parents and to Father Gregory, whose strict opinions about family obligations were God's.

College was out of the question. Not only was there no money for it, I doubted I had the mental capacity for hours of learning complex ideas and theories, or the physical capacity for drinking 27 cases of beer in a single evening.

At the insistence of my mother, who believed that public high schools were dens of wickedness and violence, I was enrolled in St. John's High School, a small Catholic school with an enrollment of about 200 students in downtown Canton. St. John's started as a parish high school, but became bigger by accepting children from other parishes, if they could pass the entrance test.

I don't think anyone failed the entrance examination, if their parents were willing to come up the tuition, but if they scored poorly, they were put in a lower, less demanding academic track. I, the first St. Benedict's graduate to go to St. John's, make a score that puts me on a mental level with broccoli.

I am excused from taking college prep courses as Latin, and some of the higher math classes. No disappointment there. I do try to enroll in a physics class when I am a junior, but I am given a course in blue printing instead, followed by a semester of mechanical drawing.

The substitution is made with the best of intentions. You'll find it more useful when you get out of high school, I am told comfortingly.

A different school administration makes amends a few years later by giving me credit for passing a physics course when I need it in order to be accepted into Marquette University. I am then a Korean War veteran.

I make the honor roll a couple of times, but my grades overall are not spectacular. I get a "D" in blueprinting and an incomplete in mechanical drawing. But my marks are good enough to put me in the top third of the class at graduation. That ranking is lessened by the knowledge I had not taken Latin or physics or trigonometry.

At graduation, the school principal tells my mother it will be a waste of time to send me to college. My mother agrees.

I look back on my high school years with the sentiment of an ex-con recalling hard time in a maximum-security prison.

From the start, my social life was inhibited by my mother, who forbade me from attending dances or dating during my freshman and sophomore years and insisted on attending football and basketball games with me.

In grade school, the only sport for which I was ever recruited to play by my fellow students was football. I wasn't very big, I never threw, carried or kicked a football, but I was a determined and fearless tackler.

I had envisioned playing football in high school, but my mother forbade it during my first two years at St. Johns, because of her fear I would be hurt. While I had grown tall, 5 feet 10 or so, I weighed less than 120 pounds and looked like I had been fashioned from a Tinker Toy set.

My closest friend during this period was a light skinned African-American, George Dillworth, who tried to pass himself off as Greek. George and I both felt inferior to our fellow students and tried to pass ourselves off as something we were not.

George had gone to St. John's grade school and therefore, under the rules of the time, his mother didn't have to pay the high school tuition.

He and his mother lived next to a whorehouse in what was then one of the last officially sanctioned red light districts in a U.S. city outside of Nevada. City officials and the police had a policy that the houses would be allowed to operate as long as there was no solicitation of business in the streets.

George described in general terms visits by some of the young whores to his bed when his mother was gone. He never did go into explicit details about what they did in bed.

We didn't have classes in sex education in high school. We learned about it from more knowledgeable boys. Not only was there no sex education, there was hardly any consummated sex.

Most of us St. John's boys and -- I have to depend on attitudes on this -- all of the St. John's girls were virgins throughout high school.

That is not to say we didn't talk about sex, or dream of it, or plan ways of getting it. We just didn't do it.

We Catholic boys operated under strict rules and prohibitions taught and repeated many times by the priests and nuns: We were strictly to avoid 'occasions of sin.' Those were entertainments and places where you knew you might be tempted to consider sexual sin as something pleasurable.

Movies with suggestive scenes, of course, could be an occasion of sin. Pinup photos of scantly clad women were not to be ogled. BUT if you accidentally saw a girl in a bra in a magazine, no sin. HOWEVER, if having turned the page, you should flip back it in order to lecherously gaze on that picture, you were guilty of the sordid sin of lust.

That was just the preliminaries. Intercourse outside of marriage was not only a very serious sin, only a little short of premeditated murder, but if you seduced a girl and awakened her sexual desires, you were responsible for all the sexual sins SHE would commit thereafter. We had a lot of responsibilities and guilt in those days.

It was a common belief among we boys that females had little interest in sex and accepted it in marriage only out of a sense of duty and a desire to have children. Most of the girls we knew did little to disabuse us of that misconception.

We were taught that sex was intended only for marriage. If you truly loved a girl you waited until then and you stayed with her and cared for her the rest of your life. After the wedding, not only was the stain of sin and guilt removed, but it became a means of gaining grace in the sight of God. Sex wasn't as free then as it is now, but I'm not sure we missed all that much.

Our classes never went into details of what intercourse was. Matter of fact, some of the nuns didn't seem to know what intercourse was, at least not in the sense we lewdly think of it. A woman friend of mine told of going to high school at a boarding school run by nuns in that period. The nuns, she said, thought of intercourse in its lesser-used meaning of conversation between two individuals. So, a posted sign in the lounge of the woman's dorm stated: "Intercourse between men and women will be permitted in this lounge only between 7 and 10 p.m."

I was a high school sophomore before I learned the sexual details. I learned it from Ralph. He told me people did it the way dogs did it. But since I had never seen a naked female, I was uncertain about the mechanics. I thought girls had a penis like boys, only theirs was hollow.

You may think me naive, and I was. Many of us were. At a high school reunion a few years ago, one of my female classmates, by then a grandmother, told me that when she was in high school "virgin" to her meant only the Virgin Mary.

So, when a raunchy boy from a public high school asked her "Are you a virgin?" she shook her head, puzzled. "Of course not. Do you think I'm the Mother of God?"

Fuck was used as an expletive by boys and men, as it is today, even before we knew what it meant. But it was rarely used in public or in a good home. It was a word used in men's bars, in the plant and in the army and navy. It was never used on the stage or in movies and rarely in books. It was never used by a gentleman before girls or women.

Given that background, the following story, told to me by a gray-haired Catholic high school graduate, is credible:

As a teenager, she gave a more sexual wise acquaintance -- a public school girl -- a lift in her car.

"You know what I want right now? A good fuck," said the girl.

My friend wasn't sure what she meant but she tried to be generous.

"We're coming to a drug store. I'll stop and buy you one."

Even many of my high school companions, including Ralph and Dillworth, who knew what intercourse was, were uncertain and highly imaginative about sexual matters.

For instance, there were many arguments and bets made about where babies came out. Many of us held to the theory that it came out of a woman's belly button, which burst open on delivery day expelling the baby. The button was then sterilized and taped or sewn back together by doctors or midwives -- that was why, in the movies, women assisting at births always called for buckets of hot water.

That theory was particularly believable because my mother was shocked when women in the movies exposed their belly button. It was wrong, she said, because that's where babies were attached when they were born.

Those were the days before sex was perfected. (That didn't happen until the late 1960s -- in a workshop at Berkeley.) Since sex was still in its early, primitive stages, it's not surprising that we were equally ignorant about the science behind conception.

Some of the strip mines near where I lived had rough, dirt roads running around them that were used as lovers' lanes. Sometimes teenagers would lie in wait until matters were reaching a climax and then emerge to terrorize the amorous couple by shaking and pounding on the car.

This was wrong, said Ralph, the expert on sexual matters. If intercourse was interrupted it could result in a deformed baby.

The basic matter of sex, whether a girl "put out" was the major focus of our thoughts and conversations.

Smoking was an almost certain sign. If a girl smoked, she was being rebellious and was likely to be liberal in sexual matters. Unfortunately, few of the Catholic girls we knew smoked.

Dillworth, our expert on commercial sex, held that girls got muscular legs by screwing. A girl with muscular legs was either an avid bicyclist or a whore.

Most of the girls I knew as a young man were steadfast in heeding admonitions against entering into occasions of sin with a boy. As late as my college years, a coed I was seriously romancing, a young woman I dated several times a week over more than a year and to whom I pledged my love, refused to allow me to French kiss or hold her in an embrace for more than a few minutes because she had been told by her parish priest that it was a substitute for intercourse.

I cannot remember when I wasn't interested in girls. In high school my interest was intense. Joan O'Hara, a dark-haired, shapely girl, was the prettiest female in the school. I stretched forward as far as I could at my desk to get a better view of her gorgeous, erotic legs when she had to write something on the board. But she was also the most popular girl in school. I knew I didn't have a chance with her, even if I was allowed to date.

I got an erection just looking at partly clothed female bodies, and there were plenty of them in the movies, that, for me at least, were far more erotic then than today's flicks that leave little to the imagination. I wanted to see what was underneath. In matters with women, I found much later, the hunt is usually more exciting than the kill.

At that time, the Canton Repository regularly printed pictures of well-endowed females in swimsuits or shorts and tight fitting sweaters. We were getting the paper when I was in high school, for it was the middle of World War II and men and women were making good wages with lots of overtime in the defense plants.

I was denied the front section of the paper where all the war news was printed. My mother believed it would be too upsetting for a young boy. (She also tried unsuccessfully to get the public library to deny me an adult library card. She feared I would read "the wrong kind" of books.)

Being denied a look at the war news was not that much of a concern to me. I was happy with the back section with the editorials and the comics and sports pages. That's where Ernie Pyle and the girly photos were. I cut the pictures out along with sizzling photos from the magazine ads so I could commit the sin of lust at my leisure.

(I went to confession every Saturday. "Father I have been guilty of impure thoughts at least 50 times a day.")

My mother regularly searched my drawers and my papers for evidence of wickedness, so I hid the photos I had saved behind a large picture of the Virgin Mary hanging on the wall of my room. I saved so many that the back of the frame bulged.

One day my mother came in my room to dust and search. She bumped the Virgin's picture and the erotic clippings exploded from the back of portrait and cascaded down the wall onto the floor.

My mother was horrified. She gave me a few hard slaps, forbade me to see a movie or listen to the radio for a month and insisted that I make an Act of Contrition aloud immediately and go to confession as soon as possible. But she didn't lay the bulk of the blame on me.

"We didn't teach you immoral things like this."

True enough. Wickedness came naturally to me. The devil had me in his power.

"I know you wouldn't think of this by yourself. You're getting those pictures for someone else, aren't you? Larry Mraz. I know it. He put you up to this. You're getting these pictures for Larry Mraz."

Larry Mraz was two grades ahead of me at St. John's. He was one of the nicest and most religious boys I knew, popular with nearly everyone at school. I knew him only slightly. He played trumpet in the school orchestra in which I inexpertly pounded away at the marimba.

My mother considered him evil because of his face, that was pockmarked from a childhood disease -- perhaps the dreaded smallpox. I never asked. But she associated pockmarks with the devil -- a sign that Larry was guilty of making me a pervert.

I denied that he was involved in any way with the sinful photos. She took that as a sign he had threatened me if I told the truth.

Fortunately, she didn't make good on her intention to call the school and poor Larry's parents.

I was allowed to try out for the football team in my junior year. I was now about five feet eleven, but if I had grown an inch taller, I had not grown any heavier. I was still about 120 pounds, light even for those times when a high school back weighed around 180.

I was slow to mature. I had not yet grown pubic hair. I wouldn't regularly have to shave until I was in the army. My voice was still soprano.

In grade school I had gained a reputation for tackling, so I tried out for tackle. I liked the sound of the position. What did I know? In elementary school the games were pickup. We didn't have positions. I had just hung back behind what passed for a line and tackled anyone with a ball -- or a rolled up cap.

If they had called my position by its proper name "rug," I would never have gone out for it. Usually in practice I was flat on the ground being run over by a dozen cleated heavy football players.

At that time members of football teams wore leather helmets and played both offense and defense. On defense I was like a glob of whipped cream trying to defend a birthday cake from the cutting knife. On offense I was a rubber mallet attempting to break open a steel vault.

Our coach had only recently been discharged from the army, where he had been fighting the Germans in France. The war was just over, but I believe he thought he was running a basic training camp for new recruits who were going to push through the Belgium hedgerows to kill Germans.

We appropriately practiced in St. John's Cemetery, about a dozen blocks from a ramshackle house, smelling of stale sweat that had been converted into dressing rooms and showers. We walked to the cemetery in bare feet. We were forbidden to wear our football shoes for fear the cleats would be dulled by the pavement.

Once we got to the cemetery we were required to run around its perimeter five times, that was something like the distance between New York and Cleveland. I was usually late for practice, which meant I had to run two extra laps. If we were competing in the Boston Marathon we could have been national champions.

Then, we linemen began hurling ourselves at a contraption weighing as much as a loaded coal car, that we were supposed to move backward five yards! It was sort of like smacking into the Chrysler Building and expecting it to end up on Broadway.

We did this in a section of the cemetery where only our barely breathing bodies had been planted. When it was dry, we raised a dust that abraded the lining of the throat and dried the liquid in our eyes. When it was pouring rain, we sank to our ankles in mud and slipped and fell while trying to make a cut. Mud was better, for we had no water to drink, there being none in the cemetery and the coach unwilling to coddle us by carrying any to the practice field.

The coach had two chief rules that pro football players today rarely follow:

  For backs: Never give up yardage gained.

  For everyone: Tackle only below the hips.

There were also regulations: No smoking, no drinking, bed by 10 p.m. and above all, no dating.

"That can ruin your stamina faster than anything else," he said. It was fine with me. I had no dates anyway.

Ultimately, the coach moved me to offensive end and defensive back. I sat mostly on the bench on a team that -- despite the tough training and the coach's rules and regulations -- lost every game, including one by a score of one to nothing.

How can there be a score of 1-0 in football? By forfeit. Most of the first string was found to be academically ineligible.

I made no memorable plays in my brief career as a football player. The only memorable game that I recall when I was on the team was in Orville, Ohio, where we lost to the public high school. The field was near the Smucker's canning factory. It was a warm fall night and the odor of fresh apple butter drifted over the field. It was a lovely smell. If only all football games could be played cleanly on an Indian summer night with the smell of apple butter in the air.

Chapter 12

Leaving

It was assumed by my foster parents that after high school I would work in one of the manufacturing plants or one of the steel mills that were busy with work in Canton. I had, after all, gotten a high school diploma that was more education than all aunts and uncles and most of my cousins had gotten up to that time. It was as much education as anyone could reasonably expect. I had served three times as much the classroom time as had my father. I had four more years of formal education than my mother.

In the 1940s, most young men, unless they came from well-to-do families, began their lifetime of work in the factory or in an office right after high school. I never knew anyone from our parish who had gone to college when I was growing up.

After graduation, I got a job in a factory that made metal cabinets for kitchen sinks and lockers. Every day I used a powered screwdriver to put in three screws to hold a towel rack in a cabinet. The task took 10 seconds. I did it over and over and over, hour after hour, day after day.

The plant had not been unionized. There was a 15-minute lunch break, just time enough to eat a sandwich and drink a bottle of pop at my place on the line before the horn sounded and the assembly line started moving again. The task was too simple to exercise my brain, but kept me too busy to daydream.

There are hundreds of thousands of workers who have done similar mind-dulling jobs every working day for 40 years. I was not going to be one of them.

I was also determined to get an answer about the questions I had long held about my birth and the people who raised me. It was a day in November shortly after my 18th birthday when I put the question to my mother. We were alone in the house.

"I'm not really your son, am I?"

She looked at me with an expression I couldn't read. It wasn't startled or fearful or sorrowful, it was more a look of quiet relief, the look of someone attending the dying of a close relative who has suffered much pain and has just watched the son-husband-father-mother-friend breathe their last breath.

"No," she said. "I've thought several times you should know. But your father. It would kill him if he knew. He couldn't take it."

My father early in the year had suffered a serious heart attack. When he returned to work, he had been relieved of his crane-operating job and made a night watchman at the plant. The doctor had advised him, "God has punched your card"

I promised I would continue the charade of pretending I was their son. And I did, long after my father's death seven years later. I did, true, tell a few young women I was adopted within five years after his death, but it was in places far from Canton and one was the woman who became my wife.

I continued the charade during my less and less frequent visits when I came to Canton. I played innocent and unknowing responding to subtle questions and comments from my father's relatives intended to draw out what I knew about my birth.

I had determined to leave Canton and its unpleasant memories long before I confronted my mother with my suspicions. I thought I might be a writer. I had entertained my fellow pupils at St. Benedict's with my stories written in response to English assignments. They were murder mysteries. I hit on a formula that's been successful in Hollywood -- lots of violence and when the story began to drag, a murder or two. Come to think of it, my mother's least favorite writer, Shakespeare, used that formula quite a bit, too. My plots were strong, but my endings were weak. Well, some movies have that same problem.

My endings were weak because:

1 - I had no idea how a story would end when I began it.

2 - By the time I got to the last page, I had killed off all my characters without resolving the mystery.

Nevertheless, my stories were a hit among my young classmates, more interested in the murders than the plot's resolution. On rare occasions in English class they asked my teachers to let me read my bloody tales. It had given me recognition I craved.

By the time I graduated from high school in 1947 our neighborhood and our world was changing. The bread wagons no longer came down our street, farmers no longer came with horses to plow lots for gardens, a few bars were putting in television sets to draw crowds. Cooking shows and wresting matches from Cleveland in black and white comprised a major part of the entertainment. A few more black families had moved in the parish. Stephens Grocery and most of the small stores were being replaced by supermarkets and our red brick streets were being paved over with asphalt.

Franklin D. Roosevelt, who had been president most of my life, was dead. But there was peace in the world for the first time I could remember and we believed there would be no more wars, now that the United Nations had been created to settle disputes among nations. Certainly, the United States, the sole possessor of the atomic bomb, would never go to war again.

I thought about what I would do the rest of my life, now that my dreams of being a fighter pilot had been shot down. I remembered the satisfaction I had received from entertaining my classmates by writing. I would spend my life writing letters to the editor.

On second thought, I realized no one made a living that way. I bought a portable Remington typewriter and began pecking out short stories with one finger until my mother taught me how to use ten fingers on the machine. She thought I was writing letters. I didn't want to tell anyone I was writing stories until I sold one. From the continual stream of rejections from magazines, it didn't look like that would ever happen.

Thanks to the newly passed G.I. Bill, hundreds of thousands of young men from the lower middle class were enrolling in college in record numbers.

I thought of trying college myself. Anything, even a return to school, was better than installing those towel racks hour after hour. My other dream was to be a playwright. I had just finished reading all of Eugene O'Neill's plays that had been published up until then and I think it was the dark side of them that appealed to me. I was realistic enough to know I was not going to support a family on playwriting, so I decided to major in journalism.

My mother looked skeptical when I announced early in 1948, that I intended to go to college. She reminded me of what my high school principal had said about its being a waste of time to send me there. I thought the principal might be right. But I didn't want to spend the rest of my life installing towel racks. Even more, I wanted to leave the small home and the almost daily quarrels, the atmosphere of scorn and fear of other races, neighbors and family.

My father said, "You're being foolish. Don't tell nobody. People will make fun of you."

He didn't believe I would leave home. I had obligations to him and my foster mother. They had for 18 years fed me and given me a room to stay in and a yard for play. They had paid for my operations and my schooling. I was done with school. It was now my duty to help put bread on the table as he had when he handed his mother his entire paycheck and been proud of it. To leave home and attempt college would show ungratefulness for all the things I had been given.

If I wanted to learn a trade, he understood. But college was for the well to do whose parents could see that their sons and daughters joined the professional or executive classes after graduation.

I had been paying $20 a week room and board since I had gotten a full time job. It represented something like half my take home pay. His wages at the steel plant had been cut sharply since he had been taken off the crane. He was looking forward to having two wage earners in the house. For the first time in their lives my parents would be lifted above the edge of poverty. The extra money I was bringing in would make life more comfortable. We wouldn't have a bigger house, but we could have a better car, one with hydraulic brakes and working shock absorbers, instead of the two pre World War II junkers with bald tires and defective mechanical brakes that we were both driving.

There was merit in his argument. I owed them a great deal. But I showed that the nuns had been right in awarding me a P in character.

In late May, I took the four hundred dollars I had saved and left the only home I had known. I knew I would never come back, except on brief visits.

I travel to Chicago to attend a summer session at Loyola University. I take only two courses, freshman English and Medieval History and find both courses to be mostly rehashes of what I had learned in high school.

I thought I might find my real mother in Chicago. But I have no idea of how to go about it. I don't even know the name of the hospital in which I was born. Besides that, I am hesitant. Finding her could dispel all the romantic dreams I have of what she looked like and the kind of persons she and my father were. No human could fill the images I have created. They might turn out to be ordinary persons.

I think she must be married and likely has children. They are legitimate, according to the ruling of society at the time. I am not. Her husband may not have been told about of my birth. A visit from me can cause her a great deal of trouble and embarrassment and reopen old wounds, which may have been healed. I fear, most of all, that the knowledge of my existence after 18 years will bring resentment and further rejection.

I walk the crowded downtown streets in Chicago looking at the faces of middle-aged women, wondering which one might be my mother. But I cannot picture her as middle-aged. I see a pretty young woman of 26 -- the age she was when she gave me birth.

I walk past Catholic hospitals in south Chicago. One of them, I believe, is the hospital in which I was born, but I have no way of knowing which one and I don't enter any of them. My adoption records are sealed. I put away the idea of trying to find my mother, although the thought of doing so will periodically recur the rest of my life. I, in the city where I began, am now entirely alone and ready to start a fresh life.

Chapter 13

The Army

The second great war to end wars ended in August, 1945. In 1948, the U.S. was drafting young men for the next war.

I no longer want to become a fighter pilot, but when the summer session at Loyola ended most of my college savings were gone. I return to Canton and three weeks later enlist in the army.

I went into the service as an immature youth lacking confidence and marketable skills. I came out knowing how to make up a bed with hospital corners and how to field strip a .45 caliber pistol and put it back together. I could also sing 14 marching songs with dirty lyrics.

In the army, I change in visible ways. I grow to my full height of six feet. In three months of basic training and regular meals, I gain 30 pounds so I fill out to a weight of 175 pounds.

Being raised an only child hasn't prepared me to live for 24 hours a day close by 30 other men my own age from different parts of the country and of different religions and political beliefs. In Canton, nearly everyone I knew was Roman Catholic. They were all Democrats, with the exception of my mother.

We believed that Jesus Christ was God, that Franklin Delano Roosevelt was the greatest man of the Twentieth Century, that sex before marriage was sinful, but that drinking, gambling and smoking were ok, as long as they were done in moderation.

We thought that people who spoke with a Southern drawl were mentally slow, that young men our age raised in white-collar families in houses that had more than one bathroom lacked toughness and fortitude and that very wealthy young men married girls whose families had little money.

Having my opinions and beliefs challenged and learning to live in harmony with those of other backgrounds is at times a difficult experience, but it contributes to forming the man I am today.

After years of my mother's bizarre discipline, it might be thought I would fit in easily with the military version. But her discipline has the effect of forcing me to be a loner. It runs determinedly opposite to the army's intention to make us work together as an obedient unit.

From Canton, I and some 30 other equally unseasoned males in their late teens are taken by train to Camp Breckinridge, Kentucky for processing. The day after, we are issued uniforms, given shots and short haircuts, taught the military method of making beds and lectured in military courtesy, that includes the correct way of saluting an officer.

The second morning I am awakened at the dark hour of 0500 by the harsh sounds of a recorded bugle. I shower, dress, make my bed, help sweep the floor and clean the latrine and line up my footwear in parade order under my bed, all before breakfast.

At 0800 hours we recruits are called to assemble in the parade ground to receive our assignments for the day. I have been up three hours. I had slept poorly during the night. I have done my household chores. I am tired. I go back to bed. At about 10:00 I am awakened by heavy booted footsteps. An older man with one silver bar on each shoulder, someone who looked like he may have been a holdover from World War II, stops at my bed and touches me gently on the shoulder.

"What's wrong soldier, are you sick?"

It seemed to me a caring question. The man is concerned about my health. It is kind of he. I feel obliged to relieve his anxieties. He might be worried over whether I am eating well.

"It's all right, sir." I assure him. "I've had breakfast."

His face reddens. He draws enough breath to fill the sails of a schooner. His head begins to look like a reddish-orange weather balloon blown up and stretched tight to its maximum size. I am afraid that if he takes another breath it will burst and the rush of air from his lungs will cause his body to fly around the barracks like a rocket until it hits a post and ends up shriveled on the floor.

"Get the hell out of that bed!" he growls.

I leap out of bed and stand shivering in my shorts while he dresses me down, using a remarkable vocabulary of obscenities. Finally blown out, he orders me to trim the grass around the barracks.

It sounds like a reasonable request.

"With a scissors," he commands.

The truth is, I modeled my soldiering after Beetle Bailey. I am slow to rise in the early morning and I regard most of the military regulations, such as lining up each knife, fork and spoon on a string the length of the mess hall when setting the table, as part of a silly game.

I acquire two nicknames in the army, the first when our company is bivouacking in tents in a cool, rainy November in Washington State. We sleep in olive drab sleeping bags that cover us from head to foot, a kind of large cocoon with a hole large enough for part of a face.

In the early morning the sergeant comes around to awaken us. I am reluctant to get up.

"I'm still in my cocoon stage. Come back when I'm ready to be a butterfly."

My reply is repeated around camp. I become known as Butterfly

Later, I inadvertently trade it for a more masculine nickname, Rubberman, a name I get from rising up from spectacular falls during ski training in the Cascades.

Army ski training is nothing like taking ski lessons as a civilian. For one thing, the army wasn't as concerned about how we got down a slope as it was in our getting up it. It figured we could mostly get down on our own. There were no rope tows, T-bars or chair lifts on the federal property near Mount Rainier where we were to take our instruction. There was also a lamentable absence of snow bunnies dressed in the latest tight-fitting ski attire.

Also, a civilian skier is not encumbered with a rifle, a steel helmet and a rucksack filled with 500 pounds of socks, eating utensils, ammunition and tent stakes. Nor are civilians usually required to ski across slopes littered with enough 5-feet thick logs to build 20 blocks of frame houses.

We are divided into two groups: those who have skied at least once (who were assigned to be instructors) and a much larger segment: those who think of a snowplow as a piece of road equipment. I am in the later group. In northeastern Ohio any rise higher than a man's head is considered to be a foothill of the Alleghenies. Skiing was not a winter sport for us.

Our base camp is on a plateau some 3,000 feet high on which Army engineers have erected several large tents held up by wooden frames.

Nine miles from the base camp, at an attitude of 6,000 feet, is Coral Pass, an area with moderately gentle slopes just above timberline where we are to do most of our downhill skiing.

An army three-quarter ton truck, that bounces and shakes us like gravel in a can held by a boy jumping fences, takes us to the base camp. On the way, we engage in the traditional American practice of making fun of the military in which we serve. A Georgia boy allowed as how the army will make us do the Manual of Arms when we arrived, using ski poles instead of rifles.

We regard it amusing until just after we arrive at the base camp and are issued boots and wide, white-painted wooded skis with leather straps and cable bindings to hold our feet to the boards. Thus outfitted, we are lined up at attention and given the command: "Right shoulder skis!"

During our first three days at the base camp, we are drilled on how to switch our poles and skis from one shoulder to the other by command.

"Left shoulder! Port!" Skis and poles off the shoulder and in the position of port arms, diagonally across the body.

"Right shoulder. Skis!" Skis and poles set on the right shoulder in military unison.

We are also were taught the nomenclature of the woodwork we are carrying and how to adjust our skis, wax them and prepare them for the daily morning inspection: bottoms waxed and facing the inspection officer, bindings in the downhill notch, ski poles crossed at a 25-degree angle.

On the fourth day, we put on our skis and begin practicing falling, the skill in which I excelled.

The instructor of our ten-man squad is a blond, 19-year-old corporal from Chicago, hardly the ski capital of the world or even the Midwest. Demonstrating the kick turn early in our lessons, he catches the end of his right ski in the snow and twists his knee so badly he has to remain off skiing for two weeks.

A couple of days later, we arise at 0300, breakfasted and, carrying our skis on our right or left shoulders, according to our officers' commands, climb the nine miles to Coral Pass up a steep, winding mountain road.

The officers' skis are carried by truck. Our skis bounce on our shoulders every step we take, the edges bite into our skin even through our jackets and shirts. We silently curse our lieutenant when he forgets to give the order to shift our skis to the other shoulder.

Three hours after we started our climb, we come to an open area in which we pitch five-man Yukon tents on the snow. They are five-sided structures held up by a center pole and ropes attached to pegs pounded into the hard-packed snow. Our stove is a square metal box into which fuel oil drips from a five-gallon can.

It works, but a few times we run out of oil and then I steal a full or nearly full can from one of the officers' tents, leaving the empty can in its place.

In the mornings we arise at 0500. By 0700 we are doing our first climbing on skis. We spend 95 percent of our skiing hours climbing. (It tells you something that when our army instructors talk about traversing a slope, they mean climbing it diagonally, not skiing down and across it as civilians do in Vail and Aspen. Traversing, in army ski terms, means stepping obliquely up a trail for several hundred yards, doing a kick turn and then sidestepping diagonally up the incline in the opposite direction, doing a kick turn and then -- well, you get the idea.)

We learn other ways of getting up a mountain. We practice herringboning, a method of climbing named for the tracks the skis leave when the boards are at a nearly 45-degree angle as they are pressed into the snow. We herringbone until, even without our skis, we walk like someone shuffling along a deck in a high sea.

Sometimes, if the slopes were not too steep, we use climbers. They are long strips of cloth with a high nap, sort of like a piece of velvet that has grown tall. The climbers are tied to the bottoms of our skis and are supposed to provide enough friction to let us slide one foot after the other up an incline. Mine, however, keep coming off, causing me to slide backward. I look like someone in a film that is being rewound.

Skiing begins soon after sunrise each day and continues until dark when, after chow, we make candles out of ski wax and string and played cards in the Yukon tents. At the end of the month-long training period, I am still a novice skier, but I have become an expert at double-deck pinochle.

Besides the basics of cross-county skiing, we practice firing a carbine from standing and kneeling positions while on skis. Unlike what you may have seen in an adventure movie, not even James Bond can shoot a firearm while skiing and have a reasonable chance of hitting the Pentagon Building —if the Pentagon was up high on a Cascade mountain.

We learn to wash in melted snow, to use our poles as splints and the skis as makeshift stretchers and sleds and to pull a dog sled loaded with enough weapons, equipment and supplies to outfit the Finnish army for a week of heavy fighting.

I think the army didn't use dogs to pull the sleds because it was afraid the Humane Society would raise an objection.

I write a long story about our ski training and send it to *The Tacoma News-Tribune*. It uses it in an eight-column spread in a Sunday edition illustrated with photos I had taken. I am not paid, but I am thrilled to see my byline and pictures in a daily newspaper. That was before I learned that many publications, regardless of their ability to pay, use free material whenever they can, if it is of interest to readers. They prefer it to paying those who try to make a living by writing.

The day after the article appears I am called on the carpet by my company commander. The general in command of Fort Lewis, where we are based, had called him complaining that the piece hadn't gone through military channels before it was sent to the newspaper. There was talk of court marshaling me, but nothing came of it.

Soon after ski training, I join the Fort Lewis Soldiers Chorus. I am prompted to join the chorus, not so much by a love of music, but as a means of escaping KP and guard duty. An order from the commanding general of Fort Lewis frees me from company duty each afternoon to participate in rehearsals. The general apparently preferred my singing to my writing.

It is the spring of 1950. I am counting the days until my discharge in early September. I have saved up a few hundred dollars and have enrolled in Seattle University. The Korean War, which broke out in the beginning of summer, will delay my plans. It was a little less than five years since the end of World War II. We hadn't yet forgotten the lyrics of wartime songs about peace ever after, tomorrow just you wait and see.

Most of us who have lived a normal life span, recall fateful times when death was a footstep away, a move in the wrong direction, a change of flight plans or the turn of a steering wheel. I shot a hunting arrow high in the air as a teenager, lost track of it and ran in a direction I thought was away from where it would land, decided to stop, took one more step and saw the heavy arrow bury itself deep in the ground where I had been a half second before.

Now, with war beginning, my life may have been spared because of timing. On June 25, 1950, the day North Korean troops crossed the 38th parallel, I had little more than two months left in my army enlistment.

The 4th Regimental Combat Team, of which I am an obscure member, had been trained to protect Alaska. But because of the war, nearly half the outfit is selected to fill out the seriously under strength Ninth Infantry Regiment of the 2nd Division bound for Korea. Because I have so little time left in my enlistment, I am passed over when the selection is made.

The Ninth Infantry Regiment fought its way up the Korean Peninsula to the Yalu River. It is the first body of troops to be hit by massed Chinese troops when they sweep across the river from Manchuria. Everyone I knew who had been transferred is killed or captured.

I have 44 days left of army service on July 27, the day President Truman signs the bill extending our enlistments for a year.

In early September, those of us left in what remained of the 4th RCT boarded a troop ship, the General M.M. Patrick, bound for Alaska. We sleep with our gear in holds the size of a two-bedroom ranch. The hold where I sleep is crowded with 250 seasick soldiers bunked in cots stacked four high. It smells of vomit and sweat.

The troop ship lands in Whittier on Sept. 9, ironically, the day I was supposed to be discharged. We travel by train to Fort Richardson, not far from Anchorage and are assigned to Quonset huts left from World War II.

We discover Alaska to be a vast land of almost overwhelming beauty, spectacular mountain ranges, awesome glaciers the size of Rhode Island and thousands of square miles of land green with forests teeming with eagles, moose and other wildlife and a countryside bright with vivid wildflowers in the spring, summer and fall.

This was fine if you are a photographer for National Geographic. The challenge it presents for a young, randy soldier is the lack of available females. The ratio of available single women to men was approximately 300 to one. That is, if we meet one. We don't see a woman for weeks at a time. The sight of a caribou drinking from a stream doesn't stir the desires inflamed by watching a shapely young woman sip a Coke.

There are some women in Anchorage, but very few are young and without a husband or steady boyfriend. Most of the entire male population of Alaska is trying to hit on any unattached grown female who isn't drawing Social Security.

Anchorage is then a small frontier city of 11,000 persons in an area that stretched for some 3,000 miles -- if you counted the Aleutian Islands. Alaska's largest city today is a modern metropolis of approximately a quarter million residents. Then it had only four paved streets, and several gravel roads. On the main thoroughfare, Fourth Avenue, there were 30 bars in four downtown blocks. Gambling was legal and people openly carried guns in town.

Women from local Indian tribes came to Anchorage in the cold months dressed in heavy fur parkas with dresses in vivid, flowery prints worn over them. They looked as sexless as nuns, only more colorfully dressed. Their attractions improved the longer we stayed in Alaska.

But Anchorage is too expensive to visit on my soldier's pay of $90 a month. Prices are four and five times what they were in the states. In the states I could buy a hamburger and a milk shake for less than a dollar. In Anchorage it costs $2.50. Beer is a dollar a glass, versus a quarter in the states. A Coke is 20 cents, versus a nickel in Seattle.

Except for occasional meetings of the Anchorage Writers Club, I stay at the fort, play chess four or five evenings a week and save what money I can. The money is for college and to help make the payments on a '46 Ford my father has purchased.

Some of the oil companies in the early 1950s are looking for oil in Alaska. In the military I had been taught to use equipment to locate enemy gun batteries by measuring the fractions of seconds it took sound to reach each of three microphones set in the form of a right triangle. At that time similar equipment measuring the effect of underground blasts on the layers of rocks below ground level was being used to look for oil.

I might have stayed in Alaska and tried working for one of the oil companies. I might have earned considerable more money and had a more comfortable life than that of the average newspaper journalist. But I lusted for feminine company and so I return to the states when my enlistment is nearly over.

Chapter 14

Studying with Coeds

I get back to Canton two days after my discharge. It is September. My foster parents welcome me back. They expect me to stay home and get a job. A day after my return, I announce I am going back to college.

"I thought the army had gotten all that out of your head," my father says.

I shake my head. Four days later, I begin my first regular semester of college at Seattle University.

I have traveled 2,500 miles to study subjects I could have taken for much less cost at Ohio State. I have done so in part because I had paid my matriculation fee to SU the year before. In part, I'm ashamed to say now, I went because it was unlikely my foster parents will travel as far as Seattle to visit me.

I also have chosen a Catholic college, as the Jesuit-run SU, partly because I am still a devout, Sunday mass-going Catholic, but also because I have begun to question many of my beliefs about God and the church and I am looking for answers to my questions.

I have barely enough money saved from my army pay to pay my tuition, room rent and books.

I find a job as a pageboy at the Seattle Public Library. My pay of 40 cents an hour doesn't come close to covering my expenses although, by today's standards, they are very little. The university holds classes on the quarter system: three quarters to an academic year, instead of two semesters. Tuition and my room rent totals $99 a quarter.

The army spends several weeks preparing new inductees to adapt to the ways of military life. There is no similar preparation to help a young man who has spent three years in the military adapt back to civilian life.

Two weeks before I began my college classes, I had been living in a male world in which contact with young women was infrequent and often difficult. I find it hard to concentrate on my studies sitting close by several enticing and fragrant coeds. It is difficult to sit for more than an hour reading a textbook. Gradually, I become accustomed to college academic life, but I find feminine company irresistible.

One weekend I have $3 in my wallet and have to decide between keeping a date I had made with Margie, a dark-haired, lively lass from my French class to see the lovely British film, *The Red Shoes,* or buy groceries. The decision is not difficult. I take the pert and pretty Margie to the movies.

For rent of $15 a month, I stay in an old, battered white house owned by the university and converted to rooms for male students and given the elegant, if misleading name of Boyleston Hall.

A tall, sturdy, good-natured and tolerant Jesuit, Father Logan, lives in a second floor room and keeps order. I cook my own meals in the kitchen; the main course often being horsemeat bought for 30 cents a pound at the busy Pike Place Market on the Seattle waterfront. Sometimes Father Logan drops in at my room to give me fruit he had taken from the residence for Jesuit priests.

There is a 10 pm curfew imposed on all residents of the hall, which I ignore whenever I can.

One morning I am about to enter Boyleston Hall after a night on the town. Just as I am about to open the door, Father Logan steps out. I know I have been caught breaking the curfew.

Father Logan looks surprised. His look changes to a smile. "Well, Joe," he says, "I see you've been to early mass."

I complete my freshman year and enroll in summer courses at the school. I am warned that Boyleston Hall was to be demolished. I ignore the warning. One morning I am awakened by the sound of workmen tearing out the sink in the upstairs bathroom.

I move to a closet-sized room in Veterans Hall, a prefab structure built to house World War II veterans and now used mostly as rooms for the school's athletes, among them, the celebrated All American basketball player, Johnny O'Brien, who had in March became the first college basketball player to score 1000 points in a season.

I see Johnny and his twin brother, Ed, occasionally. They are affable, but we are all too busy with studies and our separate social lives to form a close friendship.

Besides getting a different residence, I get a new job, one that pays better than the public library. I become a hopper for *The Seattle Times.*

The name comes from the nature of the job. A hopper hops off newspaper trucks or, in my case, cars, to deliver heavy bundles of newspapers to stores and newsboys.

It is my first newspaper job. While it is a job in the circulation department, not in a newsroom, it teaches me something about newspapers of the era.

On special days when parades were held in the city, the paper printed front-page stories describing in detail the floats and the marching bands, the size and enthusiasm of the crowds. I have the printed story in my hands more than an hour before the parade is to start.

It is my last summer in Seattle. During Christmas break, the brother of one of my friends in Boyleston Hall joins us in the residence. He is a student at Marquette University in Milwaukee.

During a New Year's Eve party, at which I go alone, he speaks glowingly of Marquette's Journalism College and of its street-smart, and thoughtful dean, Jeremiah O'Sullivan.

At midnight I kiss his date and leave with her, but I have decided to transfer to Marquette.

Although it was outlawed in many places and considered dangerous by much of the public, hitchhiking was an unreliable, but cheap means of travel for me since high school when I thumbed rides regularly from strangers in the summer in order to caddy at the Brookside County Club between Canton and Massillon. It was a more common means of transportation then. Fewer persons had cars and gas rationing and the fact that no new automobiles were being manufactured during World War II meant that sharing rides was more acceptable than today.

People who offered me rides were usually friendly and sometimes would go out of their way to take me directly to my destination. Once, a salesman for Nabisco crackers picked me up on Route 30, the old Lincoln Highway in Canton and when I told him where I was going drove me some eight miles out of his way to the country club, where he convinced the caddy master to carry his line of snacks for golfers and caddies alike.

After my brief college experience at Loyola, I traveled from Chicago to Canton standing by the roadside, waves of heat rising from the pavement in the blazing August sun burning my face as I held my thumb out. Roughly one in a hundred drivers would stop and give me a ride, usually for just a few miles down the road. Nevertheless, I made Canton as the sun was setting. Once again, most of the travel was on the Lincoln Highway, which ran two blocks from our house.

Experience taught ways of improving chances to get a ride. I learned that speeding cars seldom brake to pick up strangers. It's better to extend a thumb while standing near a stop sign. Less effective is to stand near a stoplight, but since drivers will seldom stop if the light is green, chances of getting a ride are not as great.

At night, it's best to stand under a streetlight or near bright lights, any place where a driver can see you for several hundred feet. It helps to be neatly dressed. If a hitchhiker is traveling for a long distance, a sign with the destination printed in large letters can be an aid to getting a ride.

It's also much better to be alone than to travel with someone. Drivers feel safer picking up a single stranger. Also, there is apt to be room in a car for a lone hitchhiker, even if the car has other passengers.

In the Army, hitchhiking was frowned on by the military brass at Fort Lewis, but their warnings and threats were mostly ignored by soldiers as myself anxious to get to town and unwilling to wait for and pay for a bus ride.

When I had a free weekend or a three-day pass, I used my thumb to take me to my destination -- most often Seattle or Portland.

It was on a ride returning from Portland that I decided to enroll in Seattle University when I got out of the army. A young married couple picked me up. They were bound for Seattle, so would be going past Fort Lewis.

They were graduates of Seattle U and, on learning that I planned to resume my college studies, they told me the virtues of the small Jesuit university. Since I expected to be discharged in a few months from Fort Lewis, by the time the ride ended, I had decided to apply to the school.

Several times when I was begging for a ride, the drivers bought me meals. On a few occasions, middle-aged women picked me and described the beauty of their daughters and invited me to their home. I didn't accept the invitations, not because I wasn't tempted, but because I usually was traveling to keep a date with a young woman I had met on earlier trips or had to get back to the fort.

Truck drivers were usually forbidden by their companies to take on riders, but the rule was often ignored. Sometimes drivers had an ulterior motive for picking up a hitchhiker. Their companies had installed a box-like device that recorded and timed the jarring of the truck on the road, so the firm could tell when and how long the driver stopped.

At times, when I rode in a truck, the driver would stop at a roadside diner to have bite to eat or a cup of coffee. He would leave me in the cab with instructions to hit the box regularly so it would record the vehicle as traveling on the road.

Only once, was I late for a date with the raven-haired girl I was seeing in Portland. That was not because I couldn't get a ride, but because I allowed myself to be waylaid by a carnival and a duck.

Olympia, the states capital, was celebrating its 100th anniversary. My first ride from Ft. Lewis let me off at a carnival being held as part of the celebration.

Several local organizations had booths. The trip to Portland usually took three hours. Since it was now noon and my date wasn't until 7 p.m., I figured I had more than enough time to sample the carnival attractions.

The K of C booth had a duck pond and was offering three hoops for a quarter for anyone foolish enough to try ringing the head of one of the ducks floating in the water.

I didn't want a duck, had no need of one, but the challenge interested me. My first throw sailed over the ducks head. On the second, the hoop rose from my hand and began rapidly dropping as it approached the target. The duck lifted its head as though to get a better look at the crowd and the hoop came down cleanly over it. The bird looked astonished. It shook its head vigorously and flapped its wings, but the hoop stayed on.

I had won the damn thing. One of the men in the booth picked up the squirming animal flapping its wings in an effort to escape and handed it to me. I cradled it in one arm and stroked its head until it quieted.

I named it Oglethorpe and carried it from booth to booth. Teenage girls came up to me giggling and petted it. Soon the duck and I had a small crowd of laughing teenagers following us. I fed it carnival popcorn. I had its webbed foot read by a fortuneteller who predicted a tragic ending for it.

I had a glorious time until late in the afternoon when I realized it was past time to be on my way to Portland. I stood on the side of Route 99 with a duck in one arm and tried to thumb down passing cars. I would have given the driver the duck, but none was interested in having a soldier and a big, white duck as passengers.

As long as I had the duck, I realized, I would not get a ride. I tried giving the duck to passerbys, but no one wanted it. I returned to the carnival and went to the K of C booth. More people had been ringing ducks than anticipated and the booth people readily welcomed Oglethrope back. The man in charge gave me two dollars.

I took to the road again, but the sun was low in the sky. The time for my date came and passed. By the time I got as far as Chehalis, 30 miles south of Olympia, it was dark. I stopped in a motel and spent the night alone without a girl or Oglethrope.

Congress passed a bill in 1952 giving Korean War vets who choose to attend college $110 a month during the school year. It was to pay for tuition, room and board, books, everything. It doesn't sound like much now, but at the time $30 a week was considered an adequate salary and tuition at most colleges was set in the hundreds of dollars, not thousands.

But the bill didn't cover the year of college I had just finished and my army savings were nearly exhausted. My Korean Bill payments wouldn't start until weeks after I had begun classes at Marquette.

That meant that on September 1, I am on the road again, using my thumb to travel from Seattle to Milwaukee. All my belongings fit into a battered suitcase and an army olive drab duffle bag. The duffle bag I ship to Milwaukee. I take the suitcase with me when I begin what is to be a memorable trip.

Once again I am on Route 99 waving my thumb at passing cars and trucks. As on other trips down the same highway, I am awed by the rugged beauty of the cascades, especially Mount St. Helens, which sticks its rounded white head up above the other peaks like a bald eagle sitting on the same branch as a flock of robins. It is beautiful and peaceful, giving no hint that in a relatively few years it will rain lava and rocks on the life below it.

From Portland, I head east on the old Route 30, which follows the south bank of the Columbia River flowing majestically toward the ocean. A young biology instructor at Reed College, takes me to Celilo Falls to watch the Indians fish for salmon teeming upriver to spawn. (We didn't call them Native Americans then.) Muscular males stand on crude wooden platforms that stretch into the river for a dozen feet or more. They hold nets, with handles eight or ten feet long.

Salmon leap in the white frothy water in a heroic struggle to surmount the falls. As fast as a man can dip his net into the water, he snatches a salmon as long as five feet and weighing perhaps forty pounds. He quickly dumps the struggling large fish on the platform where another Indian kills it by clubbing it in the head.

"Only Indians are allowed to fish here," the driver says. "A treaty right."

The last time I followed the Columbia River the fishing platforms were gone as was the falls, all treaty rights obliterated by new dams.

My travel takes me northeast to Idaho, where another young man drives 30 miles out of his way to show me a particular scenic part of the Snake River.

By the end of the second day, I have gotten as far as Pocatello, where I stay overnight for $2 at a cheap hotel. I had heard much about the geysers and other intriguing sights in Yellowstone National Park. I decide to get a ride north, then take Route 20 through the Tetons and Yellowstone and further east. It proves to be slow going.

I stand by my suitcase in a hot sun on Route 20 for more than four hours before an elderly man picks me up.

"I bet you were there for some time."

I nod.

"Yep. Nobody will pick you up. Not now. A hitchhiker killed a man who picked him up a couple of weeks ago. Beat him, then slit his throat. Everybody's afraid to pick up hitchhikers now. You look ok. That's why I decided to give you a ride."

He drives me as far as St. Anthony.

Standing on the sidewalk, my thumb out, I spend the rest of the day trying to get a ride going east without success. When it gets dark, I find a local hotel that will accept the two dollars I offer for a bed.

The next day, I get only as far as Aston some 20 miles northeast. I can see the twin Tetons in the distance as I stand by the side of Route 20. I reflect that they were named by a randy Frenchman and wonder what woman he was thinking of when he named them. For myself, I prefer women's breasts that are rounder and flatter.

I have plenty of time for reflection for traffic is light. I hope I might get a ride from a tourist who hadn't heard of the evil hitchhiker, but it is after Labor Day and few tourists apparently are traveling to either of the national parks, at least not from the west.

About noon, I take a bus back to Pocatello. It was late afternoon before I get back on Route 30 trying to get a ride from anyone going east.

On outskirts of the city, a gasoline tanker slows, then stops and the driver, a lean-faced man in his 30s, opens the cab door.

"I'm not supposed to pick anyone up, but, what the hell, it gets lonely."

I get in the cab and we begin our trip through and up and down some of the Rocky Mountains. There are no guardrails on the mountain highway and looking down near the top of some mountains is like looking at the landscape from an airplane flying at 10,000 feet. I get a tingling sensation in my stomach and groin seeing the great drop and imaging what it would be like if the tanker should leave the road.

We round the bend of the highway. A semi has overturned and is burning menacingly by the side of the highway, orange flames rising 10 feet above the trailer.

A state policeman directing traffic at the scene looks shocked as he sees the tanker approaching. His face becomes ashen and he franticly waves us past the wreck.

The driver of the tanker looks back at the burning wreck.

"I would have stopped, but this thing explodes."

A couple of hours later, when we calling each other by our first names -- his is Hank -- we stop at a small roadside diner in Wyoming where Hank buys us supper.

The proprietor and cook is a large man in T-shirt and an apron. There is a small patch of gray hair growing on the right side of his otherwise bare scalp. The left side of his face has scars that had unevenly healed so that part of the face looks like a wax image that had started to melt.

"How's it going Hank?" the cook asks.

"Not bad. Passed an eighteen-wheeler on its side just beyond Pocatello, blazing like hell."

Hank turns to me, "Remember I told you about drivers who had been in some sort of accident and their tanker exploded? Happened to Red here. That's when he got out of driving."

"I don't miss it," Red says.

After supper, we continue east. It is early morning when we near Hank's destination, a petroleum terminal short of Rawlings. The driver hands me two dollars and points to a nearby cafe, Ma Horner's.

"She's got rooms upstairs. She'll put you up for this."

Next morning, my first ride takes me to Rawlings. My second is with a blonde-haired baseball pitcher with the Salt Lake team.

We drive at between 90 and 100 mph during the day and all through the night, stopping only to fill the tank with gasoline and our stomachs with doughnuts. The driver talks mostly about baseball, about how players played with injuries that would have put others in bed and how everyone on the team showed black and blue marks when they took their clothes off.

The plains, as we speed through them, are mostly vast flat lands with few trees and small towns. But going through Nebraska there is a pleasant smell of newly mowed wheat and newly harvested grain.

"I don't know why I'm going so fast," the baseball player says "The season's over."

We get to the outskirts of Chicago in less than a day. We get there faster than an express train would have taken us. The home of the driver's father is there, the destination the blonde baseball pitcher has been speeding toward. He lets me off on Route 30 before going down a side road to go home.

I get a ride to Chicago. I think once again of looking for my mother, but now I am more interested in starting college at a new school. I take a bus to Milwaukee and Marquette.

Chapter 15

Joe McCarthy and I

Jeremiah O'Sullivan was dean of Marquette's College of Journalism then. All those who studied under him and the faculty members called him simply, the dean.

O'Sullivan did not have a doctorate, which has become virtually a requirement to even teach journalism today under an academic system that puts greater weight on degrees and publication in obscure journals than experience in the profession of actual news gathering. What he had was experience as a reporter on Hearst newspapers at a time when it was the most dominant and influential chain in the country and schooling in rough and tumble journalism gained as the head of the United Press bureaus in Kansas City, Chicago and New York.

He knew the Who's Who of journalism and kept in contact with local working reporters by playing poker with them in the smoky Milwaukee Press Club. He himself smoked thick, black, smelly stogies and boasted that he had gotten his first job on Hearst's Milwaukee Sentinel when he walked in smoking one of them and the editor had said, "Any young man who can smoke one of those belongs on this newspaper."

He gave money to needy students out of his own pocket.O'Sullivan scholarships they were called. He allowed any students seriously working on a book to skip journalism classes without losing any credits and he hired teachers, for the most part, who had solid working experience in their fields of news papering, writing, advertising and public relations.

I get a job as a copy boy on the morning Milwaukee Sentinel, working 4:30 p.m. to 1:30 a.m. or 1 to 10 p.m. on weekdays, depending on my class schedule. On weekends, I work the 9 a.m. to 6 p.m. shift.

I have a room on Lisbon Avenue about four miles from Marquette. It means taking a bus no later than 7:20 a.m. when I have an 8 a.m. class.

My pay at the Sentinel is 60 cents an hour. My take home wages of about $20 a week augment the $110 a month I am getting from the Korean Bill to pay for my college and living expenses. Occasionally, my mother sends $10. It is enough to get by on, since my yearly tuition at Marquette is $420 and I am paying $10 a week for my room.

My principal job at the Sentinel is to tear off the wire copy coming off the Associated Press, United Press and International News Service teletypes and rush it to the sports and wire editors.

The International News Service was a Hearst-owned operation. William Randolph Hearst had died the previous year and his publishing empire was starting to crumble, but it still had newspapers in major cities throughout much of the U.S. One late afternoon, I tear off a message on the INS machine from Randolph Hearst asking his chauffeur to meet him in front of the New York Journal-American building at 5 p.m. that day. Anyone who could use an international wire service to send a message to his chauffeur had more power and audacity than a four-star general.

As a copy boy, one of my tasks is to call the local Weather Bureau office and get the official Milwaukee temperatures for each hour of the day starting at noon. I make the call about 7 p.m. and carefully write down the temperatures on a list to be published in the paper.

But since the list is going to be seen by most readers in the morning, the paper wants figures more recent than 7 the previous night. So from 8 p.m. until 2 a.m., the last hour on the list, I make up the temperatures.

The job of copy boys and girls or copy aides, as they were called after the late 1960s, disappeared when wire stories started to appear on computer screens. For some 50 years, it was the starting editorial job for many young men and a few women, unable to afford college, who became excellent reporters and skillful writers.

They learned by doing a lot of reading and learning the methods of gathering story material. Many who became award-winning reporters were given the opportunity to advance from the compiling lists and writing single, simple paragraphs to doing major stories on national events and feature articles on Nobel Prize winners.

One of my occasional tasks as a copy boy is to take a taxi to the homes of murder or accident victims and get their photograph from the family.

My favorite job is to take a taxi to a Milwaukee Braves home game midway though the contest. I give the driver a $5 bill to wait for me as I sit in the press box watching the game and eating free hot dogs and drinking free beer until the eighth inning. Then, I am handed the exposed plates the photographer had taken of the game with a bulky Speed Graphic. I grab the waiting taxi and rush the plates to the darkroom in the Sentinel building.

In those days, papers spent freely to get a story or a news worthy photograph. The Sentinel's crime reporter, Hank Garvey, was sent to Illinois to get a story on some lurid murder. He came back by train, writing the story as he traveled. As he passed through each town on the way, he wrapped a $5 bill around a page of the story with a note asking the finder to keep the money, but to take the page to the nearest Western Union office and wire it collect to the Sentinel. By the end of the trip, lines of cars were following the train, their occupants looking to grab one of the $5 bills flying out its windows

It was accepted that newspaper people rarely paid for entertainment or sports events. My job perks included passes to the movies, Milwaukee Braves games and the ice shows and circuses that came to town. It made dating affordable, since my ill-fated date and I either walked or took a bus.

Among the passes I got were two to the Braves-Pittsburgh Pirates game. Johnny O'Brien and his twin brother, Eddie, have graduated from Seattle U. and are playing baseball for the Pirates.

After the game -- which the Braves win -- Johnny and Ed invite me to dinner with the team.

I am impressed by the good living and the freebies the players enjoyed, even down to free chewing gum. Most of the talk is about baseball and the game just played, so I have nothing to add.

I am struck by Ed's honesty when the manager quizzes him about his having stuck out on called strike late in the game.

"That last ball was outside wasn't it?"

Eddie shakes his head.

"No. It was right in the middle of the plate. I don't know why I let it go by."

I am more impressed with his forthrightness than if he had hit the ball out of the park.

There is an impression by those who didn't live through the period that the 1950s were sexless, dull, passive and regimented. They weren't, certainly not to someone who was a college student during the decade.

Wisconsin Sen. Joe McCarthy was at his height of popularity and power when I was a student at Marquette. Whether he was a patriot exposing the nation's communist traitors in high places or an irresponsible zealot and opportunist quite willing to smear innocent persons to get himself votes and personal power, depended largely on which magazine or newspaper one read and a voter's liberal or conservative beliefs.

The Hearst newspapers strongly supported McCarthy. The Milwaukee Sentinel was the largest paper in the state backing the senator. The larger and more liberal Milwaukee Journal led the opposition to McCarthy, both on its editorial page and in damning news articles debunking his claims of a heroic military career and critical of his assertions of communist puppets in the government.

My own views on the senator were ambivalent when I came to Marquette. As most patriotic Americans at the time, I was strongly anti-communist. McCarthy's claims of communists in the government and military seemed plausible, some, in fact, were proven true, but I didn't believe that men of proven patriotism and loyalty, as George Marshall, were traitors to the nation or communist dupes.

Although McCarthy had taken all his undergraduate and law courses at Marquette, attitudes of the students and faculty about him were decidedly mixed. Whether you were a supporter or an opponent could in great measure be determined by your major.

The medical and business administration colleges had large numbers of McCarthy backers who voiced their support frequently. Despite impassioned arguments pro and con, it was hard to say where the majority of Law and liberal arts students stood on the senator. Opposition to McCarthy's tactics and politics was strongest among the journalism and drama students and faculty.

I was registered as a Democrat, as were all were nearly all the adults I knew in our blue-collar Canton neighborhood. But many of my views were Cold War Republican when I reached voting age in Alaska, so I was incensed when the senator publicly called me a communist.

It happened during the 1952 campaign. Despite my workload, I am active in several organizations at Marquette. I am a reporter on the college newspaper; adjunct of the Marquette Veterans Brigade; and associate editor and contributor to *The Marquette Journal*, the university literary magazine.

Don Dobbs, the magazine editor, is a staunch and persuasive Democrat who has organized a Kefauver for President Club in his hometown of Toledo, Ohio.

At that time, the Marquette administration forbade political organizations on campus, so Don is active in organizing the University Young Democrats, which met off campus. It is as a member of the club that I take part in an imprudent scheme to disrupt a scheduled televised talk by Joe McCarthy in a social club auditorium on Wisconsin Avenue. It is all supposed to be hush hush and I don't know the plan until I am on a public city bus taking eight or nine of us students to the auditorium.

The plan, as drawn up by local Democratic Party leaders, is this:

Groups of citizens, party workers, union members, students, are to stand up at various intervals during the speech and create a disturbance by shouting angry protests of McCarthy's remarks and noisily walking out.

The object, it is explained to us, was to use up much of McCarthy's scheduled TV time and to demonstrate our opposition to the senator and his politics.

We are being given the instructions only now because it is vital to the scheme that McCarthy not learn of the plans in advance.

Squads of police are stationed outside and inside the building when we arrive. Although we are early, large numbers of people were already filing in. Most of them carry signs or wear large badges proclaiming they are McCarthy supporters.

I take a seat near the front of the auditorium with Don and Kathy Horan, a fellow writer for the magazine.

Early in the speech, virtually all the non-student demonstrators rise as a body, shout obscenities at McCarthy and walk out en masse, surrounded by a platoon of police officers.

McCarthy turns the disturbance to his advantage. "We learned in advance that the communists would try to disrupt this meeting," he tells the angry crowd. "There they go. Take a good look at them, dupes and agents of a Godless Soviet Union bent on the destruction of our country."

The crowd boos and hisses and shakes their fists at the departing men and women. We few students are all that are left of the would-be demonstrators who were to disrupt the later parts of the speech.

Ten minutes later, Don and Kathy get up and walk out. That starts the crowd booing and shouting again. Most of the other students trail after them. I sit listening to the speech that is, I admit, more interesting than the usual political address. Much of what he says is distortions of facts or reckless charges -- not too unlike today's political speeches. But his charges of traitors inside the government and communist subversion in the press make good theater that plays to the firmly-held beliefs of his audience of Midwest blue collar workers, dairy farmers and small merchants.

Some ten minutes later, as McCarthy waves a copy of the Milwaukee Journal before the audience "It says here in the Milwaukee Daily Worker..." I rise with all the assurance of an unprepared high school freshman about to make his first speech before a PTA meeting. I wave my right arm up and down in what I hope will be taken as a brave gesture of disgust, but I suspect I look to the blood thirsty crowd like a wounded heron trying to lift himself off the ground with one flapping wing.

I begin a long walk down the aisle on shaky legs. Since I had been sitting near the front, it means walking nearly the length of the auditorium. Angry, hostile faces glare up at me.

McCarthy watches me. He fixes his eyes on me and points me out to the crowd, a bird dog showing a hunter its prey. "We have another communist in the audience, ladies and gentlemen." His voice changes to a sigh, half sorrowful, half malicious, "Another one of Moscow's dupes."

Women and men in the seats shoot looks of hatred at me. Some shake their fists. In their eyes I am a traitor to my country, a godless foe of freedom, a man who would happily burn their churches, deny their right to vote and ban the American game of professional baseball. They hiss. They boo. They shout: "Fucking Red!" "Go back to Russia where you belong!" "Communist!" I feel like a New York Giant fan wearing my team's jacket to a Packers rally.

The experience alters my view of Joe McCarthy. He is no longer a well-meaning, if sometimes trigger-happy red baiter. He is a crazed demagogue, a vicious liar, a slayer of innocent babies, the Herod of American politics.

I worry that the editors at the Sentinel will hear of my walking out of a McCarthy speech, but I hear nothing and my worries are eased later when a petition is circulated by Wisconsin liberals urging the senator's impeachment. When someone brings a copy of the petition into the office the majority of the editorial staff sign it, including a political writer whose columns consistently praise McCarthy.

Chapter 16

The Man in the Family

My foster father died on May 20, 1954 as the college school year was coming to a close. He was 60 and he died of a heart attack in his sleep.

"He's cold," my mother says when she phones me about 9 that morning at the Lisbon Avenue apartment where I have a room. "I went to wake him and he was cold. He hasn't been feeling well for the last week."

She sounds distressed and at a loss of what to do.

"Have you called the doctor?"

"No, not yet," she replies. "I want to change his underwear first. You know he was never careful about that."

I had expected news of my father's death since Dr. O'Hara had given him two years to live eight years earlier. Even so, the reality of it shocks me. I feel as though I have stuck my finger into a live electric socket and my body tingles from the effect.

I had seen him last at Christmas and had given him a meerschaum pipe. That was when smoking was considered harmless and the tobacco companies boasted in colorful magazine ads of the percentage of doctors that smoked their brand.

It had been a quiet holiday, the celebration limited to the three of us trudging to late morning mass and coming home and eating a chicken dinner with home made bread stuffing followed by mince meat pie and plum pudding, all made by my mother. I don't recall any violent arguments or any jubilant celebration.

My arrival on December 22 had been a surprise and my presents had been mailed to Milwaukee.

Now that I had only a year left at Marquette, my father had taken to bragging to his fellow workers at the steel plant about his son in college, so we had no more arguments about my decision.

That didn't mean that he thought my going off to college was a wise move, or would get me any higher place in the world, a skeptical view of the usefulness of advanced education shared by my foster mother. The following Christmas when there were only two of us to observe the feast and I would graduate at the end of January, she suggested helpfully that perhaps now I might want to take a correspondence course in radio repair.

That last Christmas when there were still three of us in the little house on Girard Avenue was a quiet, uneventful time.

I visited the neighbors for maybe two hours. Mostly I sat at the large heavy and ornate walnut table that dated from the early years of their marriage in Chicago and did the required reading and term paper writing for the courses I was taking and studied for final exams.

With my father's death, a change had been made in my life. As his relatives would tell me repeatedly at the wake and following the funeral, I told myself, "Now you're the man in the family." It didn't give me any feeling of authority or increased power or even increased responsibility. With the exception of car buying, and my going to college, my mother had always made most of the decisions of the family. She would continue to make all the decisions about the house and how she would live her life.

I thought about how frustrated and unhappy my father's life had been with a cold wife who so often derided him and an ungrateful son who had left home when he was 18 and who had contributed little to increase the family income.

I took the Pennsylvania Railroad's Broadway Limited from Chicago to Canton and made arrangements for the funeral. My mother wanted the funeral home to supply the pallbearers.

"There's no point in asking anyone," she said characteristically. "Nobody likes us. I don't want to give them the satisfaction of telling you no."

That wasn't true at all. I had few rejections when I asked some of the men with whom my father worked and some of the members of the

Holy Name Society to bear the coffin and those that said they would be unable to perform the task gave $10 and $20 donations toward masses to be said for his soul instead of the expected $5.

I drove the '46 red Ford coupe back to Milwaukee after the my father was buried in Calvary Cemetery's St. James Companion Garden in the double grave I had purchased with some of the insurance money.

I was 25 when I graduated the following January. Throughout my two and one-half years at the university I had been unsuccessful in convincing its bureaucracy to stop sending my grades to my foster parents. But overall, my time at Marquette was rewarding. There were many bright, clever and attractive young men and women. We, as generations of college students before and after 1955, were going to change our society and make a better living than our parents.

I was an average student, although I did well in journalism classes. I thought seriously of becoming a novelist or a playwright. I had written a play after blowing my Korean bonus at the end of my junior year on a summer trip to Paris and London. Father Walsh, the head of the Marquette drama department, thought the work showed promise.

Many years later when a couple of my plays had been produced, I started rewriting the play. By the end of the fifth draft only one line remained from the original: "Look at how the waves break up the moon into little pieces." But the play remains unproduceable.

Aspiring novelists and playwrights are not paid wages. Now that I would soon be a college graduate, I needed to make a living.

My professors at the university allow me to take my final exams early so I can take a job as assistant news editor at a radio station in Flint, Michigan, WFDF. I borrow $35 from my mother to pay for rental of a room and driving expenses to get me there.

The job pays $55 a week. That is $20 more than the Flint Journal is paying new reporters fresh out of college. By comparison, assembly line workers at the booming GM plants in the community, many of them high school dropouts, average $113 a week with overtime. I realize, glumly, that if I fail at my new position, I can double my salary working at the kind of blue-collar job my father wanted me to follow.

Journalism pay still remains far below that of most jobs requiring a college degree, a document most newspapers today require of job applicants for the job of reporter.   In 2005 the median annual starting salary on daily newspapers was $26,000, about half the $50,000 median income of college-educated workers. Reporters on daily newspapers with at least 20 years experience received a median wage averaging $40,000.

"The reporter remains for the most part an ill-paid, anonymous drudge, lured into the work by the promise of excitement and distinction..."an old newspaper journalist, Silas Bent, wrote in his book, *Ballyhoo*, about the profession. That was in 1927. His assessment remains largely true four generations later.

Chapter 17

Sparks Stuck at Flint

Many people **regard the life of a newspaper reporter** as glamorous and exciting and well paid. In reality, reporters in most large cities make less than teachers and are subject to work on Christmas and other holidays. Far from being glamorous, much of the average reporter's time is spent in rewriting 'news' releases from companies, organizations and public relations firms or writing obituaries or covering long boring meetings and hearings.

Still in my long career there have been hours of excitement and, rarely, physical danger. I have met and interviewed movie stars and people who have had a major influence on the nation, but the first months of my career as a journalist were not a happy or an auspicious start.

In his comic movie, *Roger and Me,* Michael Moore implied that the high rate of crime in Flint was due to GM job cutbacks in the late 1980s. But when I arrived in Flint at the end of a snowy January some 30 years earlier, the auto plants were operating at capacity and were advertising nationally for more workers at high union wages Violent crime was among the highest in the nation. F.B.I. statistics show that police investigated 559 aggravated assault crimes in Flint in 1955. Seattle and Milwaukee combined reported 409 cases of aggravated assault during the same year. Canton, only slightly smaller than Flint, reported 13 cases.

A good many of the shootings, stabbings and beatings in Flint occurred in bars during arguments over women or race. The job opportunities at the auto plants attracted hundreds of single men. Most were whites, but there were many blacks and Hispanics. Large portions of the newcomers were from the rural south. Competition over women and racial tensions were intense. It was the only place I ever lived where I witnessed at least one fight every time I was in a bar for more than half an hour.

The news editor at the station, Larry, was my immediate boss. He was a thin, small, wiry man in his thirties with a pinched face and a sour attitude toward life and management. He wore the constant expression of a man who had just swallowed something too hot.

I arrive in Flint on a Sunday. The city air is gray with factory smoke, the sky is leaden and the streets and sidewalks are covered with dirty slush and melting snow sheathed with a thin layer of hardened black soot.

I spend a couple of hours at a bar talking to Granger. The next day I begin work. By the time my shift ends at 4 p.m., I have written at a furious pace more words than I had ever composed in all my journalism classes.

My days begin at 7 a.m. and are supposed to end at 4 p.m., but they are often much longer. I am supposed to cover breaking news stories, check the police blotter every morning, phone the suburban police offices and area hospitals every few hours to inquire about crimes and accidents and look in on the courts. I pick up the early edition of the Flint Journal at a drug store around the corner from the station at about noon and rewrite its major local news stories for later broadcast. My duties include covering meetings of the City Council, the School Board and the hospital board on the evenings they meet.

The station wants a fresh newscast every hour, that means rewriting the AP radio wire, an unnecessary task, since the AP radio wire is itself rewritten every hour.

The work is more exhausting than putting towel racks in kitchen cabinets, but racing time every hour meant the day slips by so fast it appears the earth's rotation has been kicked into overdrive.

My second day on the job a loan office is conveniently robbed by a gunman across the street from where I am having lunch. I get to the robbery site at the same time as the police officers. I interview the office manager and the frightened young woman who had given the bandit the money. WFDF has the story on the air before the other radio stations arrive on the scene.

That becomes the high point of my radio news career.

There was a lot of crime to cover in Flint.

One early morning, I talk to a handsome, well-spoken truck driver in his twenties less than six hours after he walks into a bar, downs two beers and shoots two young married couples at a nearby booth because he thinks they are laughing at him.

Three of his victims die. The fourth lives with three bullet wounds.

After the shooting, the truck driver throws the empty cartridges from his revolver at the barmaid. Then, he walks over to a nearby ice cream store where many of the tavern patrons have fled and fires six shots from his reloaded pistol without hitting anyone. Afterward, he casually gets into his truck and drives toward Detroit, taking pot shots at approaching cars.

"Why did you shoot those people?" I ask him.

"Haven't you ever been so angry you felt like killing someone?" He looks at me calmly, satisfied with his answer.

Too often in my career as a journalist, I have had to talk to someone whose wife, husband, lover, sister, brother, child had just been killed in a car, plane or motorcycle accident or been drowned or killed horribly in a fire or some other tragedy. It is a heavy task.

Working for the New Haven Journal-Courier a few years after leaving Flint, I was assigned to cover the wake for a 6-year-old girl who had been raped and then killed with a rock by a 13-year-old neighbor boy. The editor wanted me present to describe the scene and conversations should the boy's parents come to offer their condolences.

I stand inside the room containing the unfinished body inside a closed white casket. A photograph of the girl smiling happily lies over it.

In any wake, the intensity of grief separates mourners from the parents, wife, husband, children, and lovers of the dead person. I am not a mourner. I am an observer, paid to watch the grief of strangers and describe it to others.

The mother of the girl sits stiffly upright in her chair as she shakes hands with those who have come to offer their sympathy. Once, when an elderly woman bends low to whisper something to her, she sobs and appears ready to collapse.

The father sits with his bowed head resting on his hands. Tears stream down his face. He never looks up, even when someone puts a comforting hand on his shoulder.

I stand awkwardly in the room for two hours, smelling the heavy odor of massed cut flowers, avoiding the grieving parents, trying to look like a sympathetic friend of the family, but fooling few mourners, getting looks of puzzlement and resentment, yet no one asks me to leave, or asks my name, people perhaps intimidated by the press, maybe honored by the fact the paper felt the girl important enough to send a reporter to the wake. I am an intruder on private griefs and my painful vigil proves fruitless because the boy's family never shows up.

I feel the same reluctance going to the home of a young police officer outside New Haven, asking him politely to recount the details of how he accidentally killed his three-year-old daughter by backing his car over her in the driveway where my car is now parked. It would have been a one-column story on the inside pages, but the fact he was a policeman will put it on the front page under a two-column head. I think I would have refused to answer the door to a reporter if I were in the same circumstance, but he sits down and quietly and apologetically describes his part in the tragedy. It is as though I am his confessor and he can have absolution by telling me the story.

I am continually surprised by the willingness of people to talk about great misfortune, even when they themselves caused it. They described what happened in detail. They, the accidental, regretful perpetrators of serious tragedies, the living victims, the survivors of plane crashes, house fires, tornadoes, floods, boating accidents, rapes, shootings, you name it. They were anxious to talk away their griefs, sorrows and guilt as though their words would erase the reality of the dreadful thing that had happened, not realizing how those words would sound on the air or appear in the paper. They were not politicians or spin-doctors. They didn't have the proper words to sway the public in their favor, or know what not to say to a reporter. They were the innocents. They did not choose or ever expect to see their likeness on a television screen or in a newspaper, or their names broadcast over the air or appear in 30-point type. I felt I was an intruder on their private sorrows, but they did not treat me as one.

One crime story put me in a depression for several weeks. It too was in New Haven where I was a police reporter. It was a quiet night when the report of a house fire in a working class neighborhood came over the police radio. The blaze is out when I arrive. The bodies of a pretty 12-year-old girl and her eight and ten-year-old brothers are being carried out of the two-story house by firemen. They have been strangled by their 47-year-old father. His body and that of his murdered sister are in the house.

The story I write after interviewing the mother, who had come home after the murders, made the national news. But the sight of the dead children lingered with me for several weeks and dimmed what should have been a bright outlook on our life in the first year of our marriage, since my wife was pregnant with our first child, Joanne.

But I'm not finished telling you about my disappointing career as a radio news writer. I became Flint correspondent for United Press, a part time job that paid little and consisted of rewriting the stories I had written for the station and sending them to the UP Detroit office.

Larry was the Flint correspondent for the Hearst-owned *Detroit Times,* which paid him the grand sum of $20 a week. He asked me to write some stories for the Times for which he paid me $10 weekly. Soon, I was writing most of the Flint stories for the Detroit paper. The editors put my byline on the stories, while the newspaper's business office continued sending a $20 weekly check to Larry.

I was too thrilled seeing my stories appear in a metropolitan newspaper to complain. Less than two months out of college, I had the satisfaction of having my story about a wildcat strike at the Fisher Body plant get a banner headline on front page of *The Detroit Times.* I had my first front-page story on a large daily.

But my relations with Larry were deteriorating. It began when he started borrowing money from me. Five dollars at first that he promptly repaid a few days later. Then, he began borrowing ten dollars at a time and I had to ask for repayment.

He had a drinking problem that seemed to be growing worse. Instead of arriving at 4 p.m. to relieve me at the news desk, he sometimes wouldn't show up until 6 or 7 p.m. I covered for him until he arrived.

My standing with the station's top management also fell. In large part, it was due to a story I wrote on proposal to require local companies to hire workers without regard to race or religion.

Far more radical hiring laws are accepted as a matter of course today, but in the mid-50s the proposal put before the Flint City Council was damned as a threat to the right of business to hire who ever it pleased without government interference. The three General Motors executives who were on the nine-member council vigorously opposed enacting the law. The Flint Journal attacked it editorially. But the three UAW members who were pushing it picked up enough support to get it approved by one vote on the first of two required readings.

I write what I think is a balanced report on the controversy, but my story is considered inflammatory and anti-GM by the station management.

I am told to play down the story and ordered to phone the program director at his home and read him what I have written about the proposal before it is aired.

The legislation loses when the City Council votes a second time and the mayor and a local businessman switch their votes. But I have earned the enmity of management and I know my days at the station are numbered. Larry becomes increasingly critical of my writing and news judgment.

Not long afterward, he calls me at my rented room one evening after my work shift and asks me to cover the crash of an Air Force jet in a rural area some 40 miles from Flint. He says he is at a party and cannot get away.

I leave right after his call. Nearly an hour has elapsed between the time of the accident and his phoning me. By the time I arrive in the vicinity of the crash, the Air Force police have blocked off access and I am turned away. I park my car in a field and walk in the dark through farmer's fields, tearing my best pants on barbed wire.

When I get to the scene the other reporters and the Air Force spokesmen have left. I talk to the Air Force officers present. They give me brief details of the crash landing, and the name, age and hometown of the dead navigator. The pilot, who had survived, has left the scene.

It is less than a half hour before the 11 p.m. newscast. I race back through the fields and, after driving several miles, find a pay phone. It is a few minutes after 11. I dictate a story to the station engineer, who writes down what I said in pencil and hands the paper to someone who holds it against the window separating him from the announcer's booth. The announcer reads the story of the crash through the window as I dictate.

After the report airs, I phone in stories to the Detroit Times and the United Press. I go to bed that night thinking I have done a good job under difficult circumstances.

I get the Flint Journal the next day to read a front-page, banner-line account by its reporter on the crash. The navigator had been alive after the crash landing, his leg caught in the wreckage. The plane was burning, the flames coming closer to the fuel tank. Efforts by the pilot to free him failed and the young man begged him to take a small axe in the plane and cut his leg off. The pilot searched frantically for the axe, but couldn't find it and left him shortly before the fuel tank exploded.

Larry is furious. I had missed the horrible, but newsworthy details that put the story on the national wires. The news editor of The Detroit Times phones and chews me out for several long minutes, that strikes me as misplaced anger, considering that the paper was sending its checks to Larry, who decided to remain at a party rather than cover the place crash.

I offer no defense. I **had** missed the shocking details. My story was pale compared to the colorful account in the Flint Journal. The Associated Press stories in the competing Detroit dailies had far more gripping interest than the routine stories I had called into the *Detroit Times* and United Press.

I took stock of my situation. My pay was less than half the amount paid the announcers who were reading my words. They had more resonant voices. I sometimes stuttered. They were glib and confident before a microphone. I was frightened and nervous if I had to speak into a mike. Still, they were merely reading the words I had written after much effort in gathering the facts and quotes that made up the story.

In addition, I was frustrated by the limitations of radio news. True, we constantly beat the newspapers easily in getting the headlines and first couple of paragraphs of a story to the public. But there was so much more that couldn't be aired in a few sentences. So much more information, so many details and quotes that the public couldn't hear. I decided to leave broadcast news and work for a newspaper.

Chapter 18

A Newspaper Reporter

Most newspapers were now requiring that cub reporters have a college degree, preferably in journalism, and there were not enough journalism graduates willing to take a vow of poverty to work on small and middle size papers.

In Flint I had been a correspondent for United Press and the *Detroit Times*, in addition to my radio job. In a few years, they would disappear, or as the *Sentinel,* be absorbed by rival papers. Currently, there are more than 80,000 journalism majors in U.S. colleges who will be competing for, at most, 5,000 job openings annually in the field. But when I graduated from college small dailies were anxious to hire qualified journalism majors.

I responded to several help wanted ads in *Editor & Publisher* and was hired over the phone by William Evans, editor of *The Gloversville Leader-Herald.* Gloversville and its neighbor, Johnstown, were slumping communities with a combined population of about 30,000 located some 30 miles west of Albany in New York State.

The principal industry, glove making and manufacture of other leather products as wallets, was declining as manufacturers moved production overseas to take advantage of lower wages and retailers sought lower wholesale priced gloves in foreign countries.

But the community was located in a scenic area at the edge of the vast Adirondack State Park. It offered skiing in the winter and a wealth of outdoor activities in the summer. In addition, there was summer theater, often headlined by Broadway and movie stars, at the nearby Sacandaga Theater and in Saratoga Springs, an hour's drive away. The finest thoroughbreds, with renowned jockeys as Eddie Arcaro and Willie Shoemaker on their backs, raced at the historic Saratoga Race Track during August.

Professionally, it was a good place for a young man recently out of college to hone his reporting and writing skills. The paper's circulation was 30,000, but it covered three large counties. The Mohawk Valley was the southern border of circulation area and the northern section included the Sacandaga Reservoir area, which came to life in the summer, attracting thousands of New York City visitors to its beaches, resorts and campgrounds.

Bill Evans had studied journalism at Syracuse University and served in the Army in Europe during World War II. He was somewhere in his 40s. His salt and pepper-colored hair rose stiffly from his head like a lawn that needed mowing. He had grown a thick mustache of the same salt and pepper color to cover a hare lip of which he was self-conscious.

He had a delightful sense of humor and demanded complete impartiality from reporters in their covering of stories. He took personal interest in his 11-member staff. When I arrived in Gloversville, I found he had gotten me a clean, inexpensive room in a house a couple of blocks from the paper.

Ed Lapos, the city editor, had played guard for Penn State, where he earned a journalism degree. He was friendly, but his attitude and tone of voice conveyed authority. You knew who was in charge.

The staff was mostly a mixture of a couple of recent college graduates, including myself, and older men, a couple in their 70s, who had drifted into newspapering after high school. They stayed, the older men, because there was no pension, a common situation at small newspapers.

The sole woman on the editorial staff was Min, an eccentric, prickly social editor as unlike Brenda Starr in appearance as a woman can get without growing a beard and wearing a tattoo on her arm. Min had started on the paper as an office girl not long after the invention of movable type and had pushed her way into the reporting ranks. She chain-smoked, cussed like a longshoreman, drank heavily and on at least two occasions had to be rescued from a barrel-size trash receptacle after she fell in while looking for a discarded clipping.

Her knowledge of the world outside the boundaries of the Adirondack Mountains and the Mohawk Valley was limited to what she saw on *Gunsmoke*.

I overheard Min on one occasion taking an engagement announcement from the mother of the young woman involved.

"The wedding will be in Denver," the would-be bride's mother announced.

Min began typing at her 20 words a minute pace, then she stopped and looked up impatiently at the woman giving her the details. "Yes, but what city in Denver?" she asked.

I was given the City Hall, City Court, Common Council, education, and fire department beats. I also was charged with checking out the activities of the Jewish Center, the Chamber of Commerce and covering the guest speakers before the Tuesday luncheon meetings of the Kiwanis Club.

I used a bulky Speed Graphic to take photographs to run with my stories. Never take more than two pictures was the rule. Any shot over that was a wasteful use of expensive film. Coming back to the newspaper office, I developed the negatives, made my own prints from them and, learning how to use a Fairfield engraver, made the plastic halftone engravings that ran on the presses.

The pace was hectic, I covered and wrote about the latest events, running full out in the morning until the noon deadline and after lunch made the rounds of the beats I hadn't covered and interviewed local residents or noteworthy visitors for feature stories.

Evans didn't want to see any of his reporters in the city room reading newspapers when they had no stories to write. "I'd rather see you in a bar. That way you've got a chance to learn what's going on in the community."

I spent a day in the Fulton County Jail, then the oldest operating jail in the country, having played a role in the Revolutionary War. My stay there was to get material for a feature on life and conditions inside for prisoners.

I rode on a tug boat pulling barges down the Mohawk River to Albany, part of the Erie Canal system.

I competed unequally with 40 bright, young women who were high school seniors taking the Betty Crocker Search for the American Homemaker of Tomorrow test.

The hours were long, the pay was $70 a week, about $20 below that of the average school teacher in the area and I had to turn in the stub of my old pencil to the business office where the man in charge would measure it with a ruler. Only if it was shorter than three inches could I get a new one. But I worked with congenial people who had forged bonds together by sharing common adversities: critical readers, a lack of time to perfect a story and little cash in our pockets.

Ed Lapos and his wife, Grace, invited me to dinner frequently. Every Monday night there was a stag party at the Tip Top, a local bar at that Ed, Evans and four or five other newsmen would watch the fights on black and white TV, drink beer and play an electronic bowling game, sliding metal disks on a long table toward a target.

The newsroom held a party after work about 3 p.m. whenever someone on the staff had a birthday. The birthday of Frances Willard, founder of the Women's Christian Temperance Union, was celebrated with a boozy spree. There were parties for no particular reason held by Evans at his house. The annual Christmas party was lubricated with the bottles of liquor that had come to the newsroom during the year.

I not only had club house passes to both the harness racing and thoroughbred racing tracks in Saratoga Springs, but I could use the box my landlord rented at the Saratoga Race Track when he and his wife and guests weren't using it.

The local golf courses allowed newsmen to play free. My dates and I watched movies without having to buy tickets. And, as a theater reviewer, I was comped to the best seats in the house at the Saratoga and Sacandaga theaters.

On the weekends when I drove the 200 miles to New York City to see a play, I stayed free at the Prince George or other small or medium size hotel. The hotels advertised in *The Leader-Herald,* but instead of paying full price for the ads, they gave free rooms to the newspaper staff.

This kind of free loading was accepted practice for journalists then. The newspaper management not only knew about it, but often distributed the freebies to the staff. It was a way of keeping reporters happy without having to appreciably raise their pay.

There was an accepted code among most journalists that taking freebies and expensive gifts didn't mean you owed the giver any favors. Some journalists made it a point of honor to write unfavorably about those that gave them gifts to demonstrate they were incorruptible.

I remember an Albany journalist telling me about the great food and drinks and expensive gifts handed out at a party given by Nelson Rockefeller when he was governor.

"I wrote some pretty nasty things about him the next day. I felt a little funny, but, hey, they accept that."

Accepting a bottle of liquor at a press party, however, was not the same as taking a bribe to omit certain names from a story or write or change an article in other ways.

When I was covering police in New Haven, several times I was offered money by businessmen or other prominent citizens and asked not to report their arrest. I never accepted the dollars. What was provoking, however, was to write the story of the arrest and have it not appear in the paper. That sometimes happened and I seldom entirely accepted the usual explanation of not enough space.

The largest bribe I was ever offered was for $3,000 from a county Democratic chairman when I was working for a Gannett daily located in Newburgh in New York's Hudson Valley. It was to refrain from taking a civil service exam for a public relations post in city government so a party worker could fill the position.

I had applied to take the exam several weeks before. In the meantime, I had accepted a job as a reporter on *The Buffalo Courier-Express*, but I had not yet informed my editors. So the chairman didn't know my plans.

"It's not a bribe. I wouldn't think of offering you one, but some of your articles have helped us and I thought we should show our appreciation," the chairman said.

I was sure the $3,000 was only a starting point and I could have gotten more, could have taken the money and gone to Buffalo with some extra money in my pocket and I would have done nothing more than follow the course I had already set. But he would have thought he bribed me. I would have felt bought. I couldn't accept the money.

Most newspapers today ban reporters from accepting expensive gifts and junkets from those they write about. I cannot argue against the policies. They remove the appearance that working journalists can be cheaply bought by those they cover.

Does that mean that newspapers are fairer today when covering the news? I'd like to say so, but there's not much evidence that's true.

Editorial policy is set by publishers and carried out by editors and there are no curbs on what favors a publisher may receive in the form of hundredths of thousands of dollars from advertising or valuable broadcasting rights.

That was brought home to me when I was an unpaid local officer of The Newspaper Guild, representing editorial employees on The Buffalo News. My union duty one day required me to represent a sports writer who had been found taking money from top area bowlers to put their outstanding scores in the paper. The reporter was offered the unpleasant choice of quitting or being fired.

Management's argument was not that it was wrong to take money to put bowling scores in the paper, but that it was against company practice and policy for an individual to do it. Management was right, of course. Although I advised the sports writer to take firing, rather than resign in order to collect nearly a year's severance pay due him under the union contract, I did so only because I felt obliged as his union representative to give him the best possible counsel. I despised him for what he had done. I was appalled that a reporter would accept money from outside sources for doing his job.

But papers do sell their space. They charge exorbitant sums for death notices. Some of them charge to put wedding notices in the paper and most sell the majority of the space in the publication to advertisers. The financial rewards run into the tens of millions annually for large newspapers. All too often advertisers were given special treatment on some of the newspapers I worked for.

When I was a reporter in New Haven, one Christmas season I was assigned to go to the largest department store in the city and do a feature on the latest toys. It was a story with legitimate interest to the reader. But ë was required to show my notes to the store manager before I wrote the article. Public figures and victims of crimes don't have that privilege.

Sometimes newspapers had articles written or changed news stories because of their own special interests.

In the early 1970s I covered city government for *The Buffalo Courier-Express when* the newspaper needed to get permission from the city to install wires for its latest enterprise, cable television. There were several competitors. The mayor called a public hearing on whether an exclusive franchise should be awarded to the Courier Cable Co.

I attended the hearing and wrote a long, four-column story on it under my byline. I was shocked on reading the paper the following day to find the editor had ordered paragraphs inserted in my story disparaging those who had testified against granting the franchise.

Some added sentences disclosed that an activist Lutheran minister who opposed the franchise was "dropped from clergy roster of the Lutheran Church Missouri Synod in December, 1969. The Synod charged him with breaking church rules..."

Another inserted paragraph said this of a college professor speaking out against the franchise: "Dr. Welch resigned as dean of the Division of Undergraduate Studies at the University of Buffalo last September. The resignation sparked rumors that Dr. Welch did not leave his post voluntarily..."

Well, a cable television franchise is valuable.

The number of times facts were deleted from a story of mine or an effort was made to kill it because of the political interests of the editor were few, but they happened. They happened most often when I was working on the now departed *Newburgh News,* then a Gannett newspaper in New York's Hudson Valley *some* 60 miles north of New York City.

Following up on a local get tough welfare policy, I was told by the city manager that welfare cases in the city had dropped since the policy was announced. In checking with the local welfare department, however, I found the number of cases had not fallen, but increased.

I wrote a story that said as much.

"Why did you write that story?" I was asked by Moe Herbert, the editor, the following day. The tone of his voice sounded his displeasure. The newspaper supported the get-tough welfare policy.

"Those are the facts. I got them from his own welfare department."

"That's not your job," Moe responded. "Your job is to get information from the city manager and write stories based on it."

On another occasion, writing a story on the Newburgh-Beacon Bridge then nearing completion, I was told by the State Transportation Authority that the toll for cars would be 50 cents.

The story never ran. I was called into Moe's office. He had the pages of the unpublished article before him.

"Why did you write that the toll would be 50 cents?"

"Because that's what the head of the Transportation Authority said."

"You know we've been editorializing for a 25 cents toll."

"Yes, but..."

"Ever since you came here you've been trying to sabotage us."

"Moe," I shouted back. "It's not my bridge. I'm not setting the toll."

"We're not going to run your story."

And he didn't. The bridge opened. The toll was 50 cents. The paper never mentioned it.

Chapter 19

Editor Stories

Among the many museums in the Washington D.C. area is the "Newseum," founded by the Gannett Group of newspapers to honor the journalism profession. It depicts editors as being wise, knowledgeable and warmhearted.

I've known a few editors who had at least one of those virtues. One of them was in New Haven. He went out to dinner one evening, drank three martinis and was never seen again.

But I have known editors like Moe in Newburgh who were opinionated, dogmatic and single-minded. Trying to follow their edicts was difficult at best. Some times I didn't try.

One of those times was when I was working on general assignment at the C-E. It was a day on that two of my children were vomiting and had diarrhea from some undiagnosed illness when I left in the afternoon to begin my shift at 2:30 p.m.

I was not feeling well myself. On arrival I was given an assignment to go to Children's Hospital and do a story on a five-year-old boy whose life had been saved the day before through a rare operation involving his aorta.

"I don't think I'm the one who should go," I protested. "My children have some kind of bug and I'm not feeling so well myself."

"Well, don't tell the hospital," said the editor who gave me the assignment.

In the late 1960s, I was working as an investigative reporter for the Courier-Express. At the time, the city was replacing many of its old water mains with new pipes. The head of the investigative team had the idea that graft was involved. I spent two months investigating the manner. I talked to everyone who had any connection with the project, Republicans, Democrats, state, local and federal officials, authorities on water mains. I went to the sites where the new mains were being laid. I looked at how the contracts for the work were given out.

Everyone I talked to pointed out that some of the old mains had been installed in the last century. Most of those being replaced were more than 50 years old. There had been several ruptures in recent years and sometimes the ruptures resulted in depriving sections of the city from receiving any water for several hours or a day.

I found no evidence of graft and much evidence that new mains were not only necessary, but should have been replaced years before.

I went to the person who gave me the assignment.

"I've spent two months on this project and I haven't found any evidence of graft."

"I don't care. We say there is graft," was the response. I was taken off the investigative team.

The same editor rightly understood that Buffalonians are interested in how much snow they will get in winter. He issued an order that any reporter writing a weather story mentioning snow was to give the readers more precise information than they had been getting. The story was to say exactly what time the snowfall would begin, exactly where it would fall and give precise details of how much would be received.

A few days later, I had the misfortune to be asked to write the next day's weather story. According to the Buffalo weather bureau, a snowfall of two to five inches could be expected within 24 hours in the Southern Tier, which is near the Pennsylvania border in western New York.

I wrote a story saying so. I handed it into the night city editor. He had an attitude. It was: any order from his superiors was handed down by God, not unlike the Ten Commandments of Christians and Jews or the Golden Tablets on which the Mormon faith is based. If he had been a supply sergeant at Pearl Harbor, he would have refused to release ammunition for the guns to shoot down the Japanese planes because he didn't have a directive from the commanding officer.

The editor handed my copy back to me.

"This isn't what the directive says," he snapped. "Where in the Southern Tier will the snow fall? Jamestown?"

"Jim," I responded. "That's not the way snow works. It doesn't follow political boundaries."

He looked hard at me. I rewrote the story, making up the missing details.

The Cornell Aeronautical Laboratory near Buffalo was testing and improving devices for the airplane and space industry in post World War II years. For several years, it annually awarded a punch bowl, the size of a bushel basket to the local paper that had published the best science stories by members of its staff. *The Buffalo Evening News* won every year until early in the 1970s, when *The Courier-Express* won the bowl.

The new managing editor, accepted the trophy in behalf of the C-E. The following year, I attended the awards dinner. The *Buffalo Evening News* won, but this time no trophy was presented.

After the dinner, I went up to the man from the laboratory who usually handed out the trophy.

"What happened to the bowl?"

He looked at me and shook his head.

"You won't believe this, but we gave it to your editor and he lost it."

The trophy was never again awarded.

Chapter 20

Ann

If I hadn't been covering the education beat in Gloversville, I might never have met my future wife. She was a newly arrived science teacher, a graduate of a state teachers college in Bridgewater, Mass., where she had gone to high school.

Ed Lapos assigned me to write a feature about the high school cheerleaders. The high school principal assigned Ann to be their moderator.

She was tall and willowy and dark haired as were the other women in her mother's half, the Irish half, of the Girard family. She was also quiet and soft-spoken, like her French-Canadian-American father.

I ask if she had ever been a cheerleader.

"No," she admits, "but don't put that in the paper."I wouldn't want the girls to know that."

It was a question my readers might want answered. I put it in the story, a couple of paragraphs below the lead.

It was routine for me to stop in at the high school to check on happenings in the school district every morning. The morning after the cheerleader story was published, I stop in the school.

Miss Merritt is the secretary in the guidance office, a position she felt beneath her since she was a Wellesley graduate, as she frequently reminded everyone. She was a good source of information and usually smiled at me when she saw me. Now, as I enter she looks stonily at me, her eyes cold.

"I read your story yesterday. Ann Girard is furious with you and I don't blame her."

Beginning to feel a little guilty, after work I call Ann and invite her to have dinner with me.

"I don't think I want to." The gentle voice had a sharp edge to it.

I try to explain that my first duty was to the readers who bought the paper.

She will have none of it. I am insistent. I invite her to have dinner in a one of the community's best restaurants where I can properly apologize. After the fourth invitation, I notice her voice had lost much of the edge. Her no's begin to sound uncertain.

We have our first date two days later in the appropriately named Union Hall in Johnstown. We were self conscious at first, as men and women often are on a first date, even in auspicious circumstances.

Nevertheless, I found her easy to talk to. What I found most attractive about her was her appreciation of so many things we talked about, books and movies, music. Unlike many young women I had dated, she was not critical about the world and the people in it. She didn't allow me to kiss her when we said goodnight, but she offers encouragement. "Not yet," she says.

In my diary, I write, "I think I may marry her."

I invite her to attend the Marquette-Holy Cross football game scheduled to be held in Wooster, Mass. four days later. I think that being a Catholic girl from Massachusetts she will be interested in watching Holy Cross play. I discover she's not an avid football fan and she has never heard of Marquette.

The game is on a Sunday in mid-November. It snowed that morning and we travel more than 100 miles on slick roads, but after attending 7 a.m. mass together at our parish in Gloversville, we set off on a trip that offers danger, poor visibility and several wrong turns, but that will last a lifetime.

I left Gloversville for work on the New Haven morning paper, *The Journal-Courier*, a little more than a year later. We were uncertain whether we would continue the courtship, or gradually drift apart as lovers often do when they separate.

To settle the question, just before Christmas I ordered a diamond ring. The salesman in the jewelry store said I could have another setting if my girl didn't like the one I choose. I wondered if I could get all my money back if I returned the ring unworn. I didn't ask. I was afraid he might refuse to set the diamond if I expressed my fear that it would not be accepted. Or he might demand that I present the woman before him so he could be certain I was making a legitimate purchase, like a conscientious pharmacist checking to be sure a genuine medical doctor had ordered my prescription.

The purchase was made on a Thursday. I was to leave for Bridgewater on Saturday to spend Christmas with Ann and her family.

That Saturday I go to the jewelers just before noon to pick up the ring, that was being sized and cleaned. It isn't ready. The pleasant and helpful young woman who waits on me tells me to come back at 2.

I spend a couple of hours in Yale's Peabody Museum of Natural History, then returned to get the ring. It still isn't ready.

I go to a Christmas party being given by some members of the newspaper staff. I leave the party early after eating my first meal of the day and return to the jewelry store. It is 4:30 p.m. when the sales girl wraps it in a gold box and ties a big blue bow around it.

I don't give Ann the ring when I arrive at her home that night.

The following evening we drive to Attleboro to see the Christmas lights in the seminary there. There is an old wooden stairway leading to an outdoor altar of the Blessed Virgin. Ann tells me it is a tradition to climb the stairway on one's knees.

It's as long as the stairway leading to the U.S. Capital. She starts up it on her knees, even though it is a cold December night. I follow her. The steps are hard and icy and my knees ache. When I shift my weight from one knee to another to go up a step, the edge cuts into my kneecap. It's painful.

But Ann seems to be having no difficulty. She goes up the stairs like an Olympic athlete lighting the torch to start the winter games. Maybe she prayed more often than I, but I doubt it, because she only spent only three years in parochial school. I know women are better built for sitting than men; maybe their knees are also better cushioned.

I offer up my pain to the Virgin Mary asking that in return she help me convince Ann to accept the ring.

On the way back, I ask Ann if there is any place we can stop and be alone. She directs me to a side road just out of Bridgewater. When we stopped, I kiss her and ask if she wants to get married in the summer.

She pauses a long time. "I think so," she says. But she sounds doubtful.

"That wasn't a very good proposal."

"No," she answers.

"I'm not practiced. Will you marry me?"

She looks out the car window. Snow is falling lightly. I wait. She remains silent, pondering, then she turns and looks at me.

"Yes."

"I'm glad, because…"I fish in my coat pocket and hand her the box containing the diamond ring. "I bought you this."

She opens the box and takes out the ring.

"I always wanted to get a ring in this manner. To have someone pick it out for me. To not have to pick it out myself. Now all that's needed is for you to put it on my finger."

And so I do. She cries and kisses me.

"I hope I make a good wife."

At breakfast in the Girard house next morning, Mrs. Girard says deadpan, "Well, I guess congratulations are in order."

Ann's father comes in, looks at me and says, "Well, look at him grinning."

In the spring, Ann's doubts returned and I acted foolishly. The wedding nearly didn't take place, because I had invented an imaginary parish.

It was on our first visit to the young priest who would marry us in Bridgewater, that is 20 miles inland from Plymouth. The priest inquired about my religious background. To him I was a stranger, born in a distant Midwestern state reared in another, educated in colleges from the West Coast to Milwaukee and now living in New Haven, more than 100 miles away. He wanted to know the name of the parish in which I was registered.

Now there I had a problem. I had grown casual about my religion, only attending Sunday mass on occasion in the Yale chapel. I hadn't registered in any parish.

So when the priest insisted on the name of my parish I was afraid he was going to discover the religious backslider I had become. He would find I was not the devout, loyal Catholic I was pretending to be. He might suspect me of hidden Protestantism, an undependable, weak foundation on which a strong and pure Catholic girl was wrongly depending to help raise a family in the faith.

I thought to impress him with my vast knowledge of obscure Catholic saints. I blurted out, "St. Januarius!"

Ann looked at me in surprise. Poor girl, with her limited public school background she had never heard of the Fourth Century Roman bishop.

St. Januarius parish. I suspect if I had said St. Mary's or St. Joseph's he would have gone to another subject and would have never become suspicious.

"St., Januarius?"the curate repeated in a questioning, doubting tone of voice. "That's an unusual name for a church."

I laughed nervously and nodded my head in my most reverential manner. I hoped that would be the end of it, but to my horror, he rose from his chair, strode to a nearby desk and began paging through the thick, Catholic Directory, that lists the name and location of every parish in the country. When he came to New Haven he looked down the listing carefully. He frowned. He looked at several other pages.

There was a St. Catherine's, a St. Patrick's, a St. Mary's, but there was no St. Januarius in all of Connecticut. Possibly, there was none in all of New England.

Ann cast me a suspicious glance. I could see she was wondering about the lying suitor she had promised to marry.

Having discredited me, the priest began probing into other aspects of my past. He demanded a copy of my discharge papers from the U.S. Army on my next visit to the rectory.

My heart dropped. I realized I had another problem. When I was discharged, a careless clerk had put an x in the wrong box and incorrectly listed me as married. It was a weekend when I was handed my discharge papers by the first sergeant and the base offices were closed.

After three years in the Army, I wasn't particularly concerned over whether I was being discharged as a married or unmarried soldier. Unwilling to wait until Monday when a correction could be made, I pocketed the papers and thought little more about the matter.

These were the papers I reluctantly handed over to the curate, who I had given good reason to be distrustful of me. During a quick reading, he spotted the damning X

"You were married!" he said. His voice expressed his satisfaction in uncovering a divorcee or perhaps a potential bigamist or even a closeted Protestant before a Catholic marriage, a marriage that now might never take place.

"No, Father, it was a mistake," I lamely tried to explain.

"They don't make those kind of mistakes," he insisted firmly.

It was no surprise that he refused to marry us. When Ann's family learned of the decision, it confirmed her mother's negative feelings about me that had begun when she began to realize I would be taking her daughter far from home. From Ann's family I started receiving the kind of looks a man gets when he is accused of incest with a schoolgirl.

Trying to prove a negative is difficult. To establish that I hadn't been married ever, I got sworn statements from people in Canton who had known me for at least the past 10 years, neighbors, members of St. Benedict's parish, my cousins. I got statements from teachers and college classmates at Seattle and Marquette. I got statements from people who knew me in Flint. All of them attested that, as far as they knew, I had been unmarried at the time they knew me.

Ultimately, the curate's suspicions were laid to rest and we were wed at a mass in St. Thomas Aquinas Church in Bridgewater on the scheduled date of July 26, 1958.

But in all our married life, that produced five fine children and took us throughout North America — from Hudson Bay to Disney World, from Boston to Seattle — we never found a St. Januarius Church.

Never, that is, until a crisp fall day some 21 years after our marriage when we were driving down the main street of Naples, New York and Ann shouted, "Look over on the left!"

I stared at a large modernistic building of white cement with tear-shaped stained glass windows. In front was a small sign that said: St. Januarius Roman Catholic Church.

It is a unique and magnificent church in a striking design that invites passersby to pause for a further inspection. But then, I always imagined it would be.

I had accepted as a matter of course that someday I would marry and have children. Throughout my years in Catholic schools nuns and priests tried to interest boys in becoming priests. I was devout in those days, but I knew I had too many P's for conduct to be a priest. In addition, I don't think there was ever a time in my life when I wasn't attracted to the opposite sex.

I never envisioned that marriage and children would change my life as much at it did. For most of my life I had been pretty much a loner. One day in the army, an observant lieutenant who had the counter fire platoon under his wing took me aside.

"You're very intelligent," he said. "But you act on your own." He had observed that on weekends, instead of going to town with members of the platoon, I usually traveled to distant places by myself. He strongly suggested that I spend more of my passes with friends in the outfit.

My wife, at times, has called me antisocial.

They are in many ways right. I have never enjoyed a night "with the boys," the few times I have tried it. A stag party is my idea of a boring time

I had thought of marriage as a comfortable arrangement in which I would have more time to write, my wife doing the necessary cooking and household chores that seemed to take too much of my time. It was only a day or two after the honeymoon that I learned that Ann had different plans for our married life.

I soon discovered that living with another person and, not long after, raising children takes up an enormous amount of time, far more than the single life. I'm not the first man to discover that and I'm amazed after nearly 50 years of marriage to Ann that I was ever so naive.

And yet, it is the best and most rewarding thing I have accomplished. Marriage gives most women and men something cherished and unique -- their own children. But with me, my wife and children are particularly special. I have a family at last. My only real family -- with all the conflicts, tears, disappointments, pride, joys, regrets and rewards that brings.

I am delighted with the unique beings that are a part of me, even when living their own separate lives.

Our first child, Joanne, was born a year after we were married when I was working in New Haven. Our second child, Michael, was born in New York City when I was assistant news director at Fordham University. Our third child, Robert, was born in Newburgh. The last two, Jonathan and Margaret, were born in Buffalo, where I was to be a journalist for 30 years.

They are grown now and have productive and fulfilling lives. They have contributed much to the communities in which they live. They are engineers and technicians and important wheels in management's of large corporations. Joanne is an occupational therapist. Margaret, our dare devil daughter, earns a living in Vail as a white water rafting guide, ski instructor and volleyball coach.

We have grandchildren who show promise of reaching or surpassing the levels of their parents. They will have the usual growing up doubts of who they are.

But when my children and my grandchildren trace their roots on my side of the family they end with me. I take pleasure in that knowledge.

Chapter 21

The Despised Poor

I had first covered a few of Rockefeller's appearances when I began working on the *Newburgh News* in 1961.

I started there as a reporter just before it made national news because of its harsh welfare Reform program.

The Newburgh welfare controversy sprang from the widespread belief in the community that the city's economic decline was being caused largely by the migration of blacks into the city. The expressed reasoning was that the blacks had come from the South to the Hudson Valley intending to live comfortably on the rich benefits afforded by the states welfare program.

It was not a belief unique to Newburgh, but no community ever tried such harsh measures to try to cut benefits to the poor.

The city administration announced a policy that limited anyone other than the aged, the blind and the handicapped to three months of welfare a year.

The restriction largely applied to mothers and their children, the aid category in which African Americans represented the majority of recipients.

It also would cut mothers of "illegitimate children" from the welfare rolls if they should have any more children out of wedlock and restricted newcomers to the city to 60 days of welfare payment Ñ but only if they could prove they came because of a concrete job offer. If not, they could receive aid for only two weeks.

And it would have published the names of welfare recipients in the newspaper and hung them on community bulletin boards.

The policy was announced by the new city manager, Joseph McDowell Mitchell, who was hired by the Republican City Council only a few months before I came to Newburgh as a newspaper reporter.

The Maryland born and bred Mitchell had been given the task of cutting the welfare rolls, with the hoped for result of driving newly arrived blacks from the small city of 31,000.

Mitchell's first action was to require that welfare recipients report to the police station and be photographed and interrogated before picking up their welfare checks.

I had developed contracts in the New York City press though my job as assistant news editor at Fordham. I began writing about what the city was trying for the then liberal *New York Post* as well as for *The Newburgh News.*

It soon became a national story. Mitchell's program was declared unlawful by the state and a fight began in the courtroom and in the press.

Said *The Wall Street Journal*: "Newburgh has shown one way a community can meet its obligation to those who need help without abusing those who need help."

Said *The New York Times*: "Newburgh, enjoying know-nothing applause from near and far for "getting tough" on the needy, must be made by the state to realize that it is not a law unto itself."

The Newburgh News, its editors and most of its reporters strongly supported Mitchell's program, reflecting the general mood of the community.

As the story grew, in addition to the *New York Post*, I began working as a stringer for the *New York Herald-Tribune.* If a story broke in the morning, I called The Post for its afternoon edition. If it was afternoon, I called my story into the morning Herald-Tribune and tried for a different angle or new facts for the Post.

I also wrote long pieces on the controversy for the Associated Press and *The London Sunday Express.*

I continued my reporting on the rumpus and its results on the community even after *The Newburgh News* management took me off the story. It felt I should restrict my reporting to writing only what Mitchell had to say about the controversy.

One of my stories was published, as usual, without my byline, on the front page of *The Herald-Tribune.* That morning I was asked by the city editor of *The Newburgh News* to rewrite the *Herald-Tribune* for the afternoon edition, so I ended up rewriting my own story unbeknownst to my editors.

Ultimately, Mitchell's effort at welfare "reform" was proved to be illegal or useless. No able-bodied welfare cheats were found, the city continued to lose old industry and, partly because of the welfare reputation the community had received, new industry was reluctant to come to Newburgh. Because the city cut payments to the local hospital for welfare recipients, the hospital had to raise its fees for patients who could pay. The caseload of the local Catholic Charities office doubled and its budget rose 75 percent.

Taxes in Newburgh continued to rise. As for Mitchell, he was kicked out of the International City Managers Association for open politicking, was indicted for bribery involving zoning regulations, and disappeared from public view after a brief farcical career as field director in Virginia and Maryland for the segregationist White Citizens Council.

(So many liberals infiltrated Mitchell's "model Maryland chapter" in Prince George's County that it ultimately voted to merge with the local chapter of the heavily black Congress of Racial Equality.)

The resulting book I wrote, *The Despised Poor: Newburgh's War on Welfare,* got favorable reviews in newspapers and in national magazines as *The Atlantic* and *The Saturday Review of Literature. The New York Times* reviewer said it "provides a calm, coherent and carefully documented narrative."

But there was little interest in the public on the subject and its publisher, Beacon Press, didn't have the resources to do much promotion.

It did pay my expenses to travel to Chicago to appear on Kup's Korner, a syndicated talk television talk show hosted by Chicago Sun-Times columnist Irv Kupcinet. The other guests included heavyweight boxing champion Muhammad Ali; Ted Sorensen, special counsel to President Kennedy, whose book, *Kennedy,* had recently been published; George Plimpton, publisher of *The Paris Review* and a best selling author on sports; Raymond Motley, one of President Franklin D. Roosevelt's advisors and Newsweek columnist; and Alan Watts, an authority on Zen Buddhism.

On this trip to Chicago, I again looked into the faces of middle-aged women walking on Michigan Avenue wondering if any of them could be my mother. But I made no attempt to find her. I thought of her and wondered if she still lived in the city and would see the telecast.

My one experience with a bookstore autographing session was a disaster.

I convinced my publisher that it would be a good idea if I traveled 400 miles to Newburgh and autographed some of my books at the Hudson Valley Book Store there.

The person I spoke to at Beacon Press said someone there would make the arrangements.

I take a Monday off from work and fly to Albany the day before. I stay overnight with the family of a former fellow reporter at the *Newburgh News,* Jack Devine, who is now doing public relations for the State Transportation Authority.

I borrow one of Jack's cars the next day, drive to Newburgh and get a room in the Newburgh Hotel on Broadway, across from the book store, then visit with friends until after midnight. I return to the hotel and find the entrance door locked.

I knock loudly, several times. It is several minutes before a sleepy man with a couple days beard comes to the glass door and inspects me.

"The door's locked," I announce, in case he doesn't know that.

He nods.

"I'm a guest here. I need to get in."

He looks at me for a long time. "We always lock the door at midnight." He says the words slowly in a tone that suggests that it is common practice to lock hotel doors at midnight. Finally, he grumbles under his breath and reluctantly opens the door. I go to my room and to bed.

At 5 a.m., a loud banging that seems to come from someplace next to the bed awakens me. By first thought is that a steam boiler somewhere in the bowels of the hotel is about to explode. Threatened explosion or not I'm not going out of my room in my underwear. I frantically start dressing. I'm tying my right shoe before I realize that someone is hitting the water pipe with a hard object.

I find out later that a large party had taken several rooms on the floor below. Since there were no telephones in the rooms, one member of the party was banging on the water pipe to awaken the rest of the group.

Since I'm dressed, I decide to check the car, parked on the street near the hotel. It has a $20 ticket on it for illegal parking.

I toddle to the police station.

"We ticket cars if they're parked on the street after midnight," the desk sergeant says in the same tone of voice as the hotel janitor.

I pay the fine, have breakfast and read in my room until 9 a.m. when I cross the street to the bookstore. I am happy to see copies of my book in the window, but there is a sign on the door: "Closed on Mondays."

No one had told the store I was coming. If anyone was desperate for a copy of my book, they were going to have to break a very large window.

I drive back to Albany and cheer up a bit at dinner with the generous Devines. Afterward, Jack drives me to the airport and says goodbye.

When I check in with the airline, it has no record of my reservation. The plane is full and there are no further flights to Buffalo that night.

I remain determined that I will autograph my book to buyers in Newburgh. A month later, I again make the trip to the Hudson River city. This time I have taken the precaution of notifying the bookstore owner myself in advance. The bookstore has an ad in the paper announcing my coming arrival. When I happily stride into the store on the appointed day, the owner greets me apologetically.

"I hate to tell you this," he says, "but the books I ordered didn't come. I have only four copies."

I never went back.

Chapter 22

Contacts with the Mafia

The book was largely finished when I became a reporter for *The Buffalo Courier-Express* in July, 1964.

We bought a three-bedroom ranch on nearly two acres of land in the suburb of Hamburg, about 10 miles south of Buffalo. The road on which we live had only a dozen houses when we bought the house for $18,000. The surrounding land was farmer's fields and woods. Houses have been built on much of what was open land but the woods remain and we still occasionally see deer and wild turkey.

On our land, we have added fruit trees, and trees of many other varieties, blueberries, flowers and, when the children were with us, a large vegetable garden. I also dug a pond that we stocked with ducks until I grew tired of the foxes eating all of them every winter. After that, we stocked it with gold fish, that the herons ate every summer.

I was to spend a total of 30 years as a journalist in Buffalo, most of the time impersonating a reporter. I covered beats and stories from the auto factories to the zoo -- a fairly common experience for most journalists. But one unexpected story not on my regular beat was to cause me to be exposed to a lot of criticism from my fellow journalists.

From time to time, I tell the story of how I slipped into the house of a Mafia godfather, Stefano Magaddino.

Magaddino was one of the original members of the Mafia's governing commission. In Western New York, he headed a crime family that controlled illegal gambling, prostitution, loan sharking, labor racketeering and other crimes in an eastern Great Lakes area in which Buffalo, Niagara Falls and Hamilton, Ontario where the major cities.

On a cold and rainy Nov. 30 in 1968, Magaddino was scheduled to be arraigned on charges of international racketeering and conspiracy to commit a crime. Because his doctor said a heart ailment made the 77-year-old Mafia godfather unable to appear in court, federal authorities agreed to hold the arraignment in his home and to limit news coverage to one reporter, who would give his account of what happened inside the house to the other journalists waiting outside.

I came to work that day at 2:30 p.m., expecting to cover a business or labor story. At 5, Scott Hayden, the assistant managing editor, asked me to go to Magaddino's house and cover the arraignment. The house was near Lewiston, an upscale community 10 miles east of Niagara Falls. Hayden said if I saw Joe Wilhelm, the paper's Niagara Falls reporter, to tell him I was covering and that he was to cover his common council meeting.

So far it was a simple, fairly routine assignment. What the editor said next took it out of the routine category. He advised that there would be a pool reporter, who would be the only reporter authorized to enter the house. However, he continued, the *Courier* had not agreed to the pool. He urged me to get in the house.

I left the office with the grim realization that I had just been strongly encouraged to get into the occupied home of a top Mafia chieftain, who didn't want me there. Not only would he and his family and associates object to my presence, so would the police and court officials and the other journalists.

It was on my mind during the hour it took to drive to Lewiston in the car of Iggi Sorgi, the photographer who was to snap the scene outside the house.

Magaddino's large stone ranch house was at the end of Dana Lane, a cul-de-sac with the homes of his brother and son-in-law at the beginning of the street, acting as an informal checkpoint for any vehicle entering the development.

In the dark, and in a strange and remote section of Niagara County, Sorgi and I had a hard time finding Dana Lane. When we did, we found the lane blocked by a state police car.

The trouper said Wilhelm was at the scene and refused to let the car go further, despite my insistence I was assigned to cover the story. Leaving Sorgi with the car, I went ahead on foot, bypassing the trooper.

Arriving at the Magaddino home, I saw mostly police and television news vehicles. I couldn't find Wilhelm or any other reporters. I later learned they were in some of the parked cars and vans, keeping warm.

Noticing a man carrying a black case walking up to the door, I catch up with him and walk a foot or two behind. James V. LaDuca, Magaddino's son-in-law, opens the front door.

"Come in, doctor," LaDuca says to the man in front. I walk in just behind the doctor. Apparently believing I was with the doctor, LaDuca lets me in the house.

There are three women in the living room, two of them in their thirties or early 40s and a stout, white-haired woman. They all glare at me with their dark eyes. Their silence and their expressions tell me as much as words that I am not wanted; I imagine they think I am a federal agent, or a lawyer for the government, someone who represents an old family enemy.

The doctor has disappeared down a hallway that leads to Magaddino's bedroom. The house is far from palatial. I had expected something more imposing, but it was as deep as it was wide, so it is bigger overall than it appears from the street.

I walk toward the back of the house into the kitchen where I find Cliff Spieler from the Niagara Falls Gazette who is the pool reporter. He is sitting with a half dozen federal agents. Spieler, about 40 with thin, sandy hair and wearing horn-rimmed glasses, looks surprised. He pulls me aside and informs me pompously that he had been selected as THE pool reporter and HE was the only reporter supposed to be covering the story.

"Is that so?" I say.

Neil J. Welch, special agent in charge of the Buffalo FBI office, pops into the kitchen.

"Do I know you?" He sticks out his hand.

I shake his hand and remind him we had met several months before when I had been covering a couple of bank robberies. He walks away and exits the kitchen.

A few minutes later, he returns. "You know there's only pool coverage?" he says in a low, confidential voice. "The Gazette is providing coverage."

"Is that right?" I say. "Where is the arraignment going to be held?"

"Right here, in his bedroom."

I nod. My experience is that few people in authority will see that a reporter is physically removed from a scene, if he insists on remaining where he is.

So I remain in the kitchen and no more is said. A few minutes later, the federal people and the Gazette reporter begin filing into the hallway that leads to Magaddino's bedroom. I stay in the kitchen until everyone else has left and then follow the dozen or so men.

Two federal agents stand blocking the bedroom doorway.

"Excuse me," I say. They step aside and I enter and stand just inside the room, near the door, so that, with the exception of Magaddino, the participants have their backs to me.

LaDuca stands at the foot of the bed and protectively and politely reminds those present that smoking is not permitted.

Magaddino was a small, balding man and what little hair he had left was white. I don't think his feet would have reached much more than halfway to the foot of the king-sized bed if he were fully stretched out. Just then, he lay under a white satin spread with his head propped up by two large pillows, wearing lime-colored pajamas.

He was freshly shaved and his face was slightly red. His head was like a forgotten apple that had paled and shriveled with age and grown moldy on top. At the foot of his bed was a large statue of the Infant of Prague and a small television set. On the right side of the headboard was a statue of the Virgin Mary. I could picture him as he might be at his wake with a rosary clasped in one hand, a crucifix propped up in the coffin near his head.

Now, an oxygen tank stood next to Mary's statue in the bedroom.

As Commissioner Maxwell read the charges against him, Magaddino's face grew redder, but he had only a few words to say.

"Tell it to my attorney," he growls in a low, rasping belligerent voice.

He raised his head from the pillows only once Ñ to put on his reading glasses and sign the $50,000 bail bond supplied by the Cosmopolitan Mutual Insurance Co. of New York City.

I don't take notes. I am afraid the action will be noticed and someone, U.S. Commissioner Edmund F. Maxwell, who was conducting the arraignment, or Welch or maybe Magaddino himself will order me out of the room.

I stay and concentrate on what is being said and the surroundings. When I am back in Sorgi's car, I can write it all down in a notebook, while the details were fresh.

The arraignment takes less than five minutes. When it is over, the FBI wants to fingerprint Magaddino. His attorney, Joseph P. Runfola, objects.

"My client is too ill," he says.

"I don't think it will hurt him. All we're going to do is hold his hand," Welch replies.

Outside the house, the reporters and television cameramen crowd around Spieler to hear his account of what happened inside.

His first angry words are: "The Courier broke the pool agreement. The Courier broke the agreement!" He shouts it over and over, pointing at me.

I face a choleric night city editor, Jim Cleary, when I get back to the office to write my story. Spieler had called the paper and charged the newspaper and me with unethical conduct in breaking an agreement made in good faith.

Cleary is unaware of the managing editor's instructions to me. As far as he is concerned, I have embarrassed the newspaper.

"The story's going on the front page, but you're not going to get a byline," he says. It is the ultimate punishment in his mind.

Considering the possibility that Magaddino and his family and associates might be annoyed if they knew I had gotten into the house on a false pretense, I am relieved to hear it.

I got to know another figure connected to the Mafia on a friendlier basis.

Ron Fino was the son of one of Magaddino's lieutenants. His father, Joseph Fino, for a time headed the Buffalo branch of the godfather's organization. For most of the time I knew him, Ron was business manager of the mob-dominated Local 210 of the Laborer's Union. In appearance and manner, the black-haired younger Fino was more like Peter Falk, than Al Pacino, despite a nose broken twice in sparring matches with boxers in Skillman's Gym when he was young.

The public and his associates regarded the union leader as part of the Mafia. I knew him as a rich source of information when I covered labor for *The Buffalo News*. I also knew that he was giving much of his information, not only to me, but also to the FBI.

It may be that Ron and I hit it off because we had several things in common. My foster father was of Sicilian ancestry, as was his. Ron's mother had been of Irish-German descent. My foster mother was also half Irish. I had relatives who were rumored to be part of organized crime.

The strongest tie might have been that both of us were products of Catholic schools. We didn't believe that gambling and drinking by themselves was sinful.

Nevertheless, our religious attitudes were different. I had stopped going to mass on a weekly basis. I had come to doubt some tenents of the faith as the virgin birth and the belief that the Bible was written by God. Still, many of my actions were based on what I had learned in Catholic schools. I believe in the importance of telling the truth, in aiding the poor and the wrongness of killing and hurting others.

I believe in the possibility of something greater than man, but if there is a God he is the God of mercy and kindness who created a heaven for all. I am proud I belong to the church of Michelangelo, Da Vinci, Dante and Graham Greene.

Fino's faith was based more on belief of magical powers that he was convinced the saints possessed. He practiced a daily ritual of reciting all the saints names he could remember, then blessing himself with holy water from the Lourdes shrine in France, saying three Hail Marys, one Our Father, a brief Act of Contrition and repeating nine prayers to St. Jude. He ended the ritual by declaring: "I believe in God."

It's not too much of a stretch to believe Ron's schooling and his motherÕs strong religious beliefs were determining factors in his decision to be an informant, first for the CIA, later for the FBI.

ÒI was in the navy just out of high school, full of patriotism and doing good things the brothers and the nuns and my mother taught me. And, I guess the feds knew all about my father, what he did, because one day I'm in a classroom learning about how to splice a wire and I'm called out and this CIA agent is waiting for me, Harold Stone. We ride around in his car and he wants me to ask my father if he knows Sam Trafficante down in New Orleans. They want to know if Trafficante was involved in the Kennedy assassination. So that's how I got involved in the first place and I felt honored to look into something as important as the assassination of a president."

Fino told me that story during one of our long conversations over lunch in Buffalo's Hotel Lenox.

He told of well-known national politicians who had accepted donations from his associates in the Mafia. His Catholicism didn't extend to being faithful to his wife. He was involved with a former Playboy bunny and told me of pressure put on the women in the club to have sex with visiting celebrities and important local politicians, including a well-known Republican congressman.

That information and much of other things he told me couldn't be published, since it was based on hearsay. But I did receive much information that made the paper, even if some of it was background.

Our lunches ended when the Mafia discovered Fino's role as an informer and put out a $500,000 contract on him. He called me at home from Oklahoma when he was fleeing to suggest I write a book on his life.

I think Ron's reactions to his associates discovering his long run as an informer ranged from terror to relief. I wasn't the only one in the press that knew his secret. I think he wanted to be found out. He wanted to be known as a good guy. His children were in Catholic high schools and he may have wanted subconsciously to relieve them of the burden of having a father whom the public associated with organized crime.

My wife demanded that I tell Fino not to call our home again. But I did agree to meet him to gather material for a possible book.

I was worried that someone looking to collect the contract on Fino might follow me to his hide out. Since my beat was the local automotive industry as well as labor, it was not difficult to get Ford to loan me a new automobile with Michigan plates, although it violated the newspaper's directives.

One weekend I drove to Danvers Mass., north of Boston, an area where the Irish Mafia ruled organized crime and the FBI thought it a good place to hide an informer on La Costa Nostra. I spent two days with Ron near the ocean and I recorded 12 hours of conversation about his family, his background and the mob.

Two weeks later I again drove to Danvers and did another 12 hours of recording. But I found no publisher interested in the proposed book. Too many books had already been written about too many Mafia informers and Fino's name was unfamiliar in New York City, where they had their offices.

I dropped the idea for the book. The last I heard, Fino was lecturing FBI agents and trainees in Washington, D.C.

Chapter 23

The Guild

I'm a union man. Have been since I was a teenager and one of the nuns in my high school invited a labor priest to talk to the class about the need for unions in a capitalist society.

My father knew nothing about the philosophical background behind the formation of unions. Neither Father Gregory nor any of my teachers up until then had mentioned the papal encyclicals that not only supported and encouraged the formation of labor unions, but talked of workers having an obligation to their fellow men and women to join them in order to obtain a living wage and just working conditions.

I first joined the Newspaper Guild in Milwaukee in 1953. Later I became president of the small local representing editorial employees at the Newburgh News.

In 1973, I was elected to the unpaid but demanding post of president of the Buffalo Newspaper Guild, a responsibility I took on in addition to my job as reporter.

The BNG represented nearly 500 employees of *The Courier-Express*, the rival *Buffalo News* and a suburban daily, *The Tonawanda News*. It represented the reporters, editors and photographers on all three papers as well as drivers and other members of the circulation department on the *Courier* and some advertising workers on both the *News* and *Courier*.

At the time I was president, both the *Courier* and the *News* were family-owned newspapers and the hourly wages of reporters were the second highest in the nation, outside of New York City.

We negotiated with men who were honest, fair and genuinely concerned about the welfare of the staff in a cordial, if smoky, atmosphere. Even so, unions must have some sort of power, if negotiations are to be conducted on an equal basis.

Even the most generous general manager must be able to say to the paper's owners that he was successful in obtaining labor peace though his concessions. If labor peace is already guaranteed during the talks, there is less incentive for management to grant higher wages and increased benefits.

In the 1970s, it was still possible for unions to mount a successful strike, particularly at the *Courier*, where we had the drivers of the delivery trucks in the union.

So it was that when I was president of The Buffalo Newspaper Guild we had strike authorization at all three papers when we went into negotiations for a new contract. I knew very well that our members would never support an actual strike, but management had to think it was possible. Power is mainly an illusion. You have it -- if the other side thinks you have it.

The word strike was never mentioned at the bargaining table. To make such a threat would have polluted the atmosphere and worked against an agreement. It would have issued a challenge. People don't respond well to expressed challenges. They are inclined to stiffen their stand.

I did discreetly inquire about the cost of printing strike signs at printers who had business with the publisher. An upstairs room was rented above a tavern that faced the *News* building with the purpose of possibly making it a strike headquarters. But the word strike was never mentioned at the bargaining table.

We signed a contract for a 12 percent wage increase over two years and increased pension benefits at the *Courier* by a third.

Nevertheless, I found some union members could be ungrateful and vindictive.

Management refused to include those who were already 65 or older from receiving the additional benefits, saying it couldn't afford the costs. We did, however, succeed in getting an additional $100 a month for the older members.

One editor who was over 65 was furious with me, even though he got an extra $100 every month when he retired a year or two later.

Joseph P. Ritz

When *The Courier*, which had been sold to the Cowles Corp, folded in September of 1982, he wrote me a note: "I'm glad you're out of work. I hope you never find a job."

Chapter 24

Fewer Opportunities Now

There are 253 fewer daily newspapers in the United States than when I got out of college in 1955. Competing independently-owned daily newspapers have virtually disappeared. So have family owned newspapers. And, although the U.S. population has grown by 100 million since 1955, the combined circulation of daily newspapers Ñ 56 million Ñ is about the same as it was when I began my career.

The Milwaukee Sentinel was sold to the competing *Journal* in the early 1960s. By then, *The Detroit Times* had folded. *The New York Herald-Tribune* and *The Newburgh News* are gone. *The New York Post* has been on the brink of death several times in the last decade. It is tottering as I write this.

But until September of 1982, I had never been on the staff of a newspaper when it died.

It was a shock, but not a surprise when *The Buffalo Courier-Express* folded.

I learned the paper was in trouble in the final months of my term as president of the Guild local. In the spring of 1975 I received a call from Bob Kopp, the lawyer who had negotiated the contract for the paper, asking the union to forego a 3.8 percent wage increase due the membership.

The company opened its financial records to an accounting firm representing the Guild. Most newspapers lose money early in the year, but more than make up the loss during the ad-heavy Christmas season. The figures our accountants saw told us that the loss for the early part of the year was greater than expected and the anticipated Christmas ads would not make up for the loss.

In 1974 the *Courier* had gone into the red for the first time in modern times, with a loss of $84,000. In the first two months of 1975, the paper had hemorrhaged red ink totaling $477,000, more than twice its loss during the same period two years before. If the trend continued, even though the paper would make a profit in the pre-Christmas months, the *Courier* would lose a million dollars.

The paper's daily circulation had dropped from 165,000 in the 1950s to 116,000, despite an increase in area population. The Sunday circulation had fallen from 312,000 a decade earlier to 270,000. Advertising lineage for 1974 was down 6.7 percent and the first two months of 1975 showed a drop of 8.5 percent from January and February the previous year.

All the Guild leaders, myself included, went before the membership and asked that the wage increase be foregone. The vote to give up the pay raise was overwhelmingly in favor.

In the years to come, Guild members were to accept wage increases of 2 to 3 percent annually — far below the cost of living, which was to rise 61.3 percent from 1975 through 1982.

These sacrifices would not be enough to save the paper. Most of *The Courier's* advertising revenue came from its thick Sunday paper. *The News*, which had no Sunday paper, made its profits Monday through Saturday. The Connors family, which owned the *Courier*, and the Butler family, which owned *The News,* were content with that arrangement for decades.

In 1977, investor Warren Buffet, "the sage of Omaha," who had bought *The Buffalo News* for $34.8 million, started a rival Sunday paper that he sold for 30 cents — 20 cents less than the Sunday Courier.

Two years later the Connors sold the paper and the TV cable operation to The Minneapolis Star-Tribune Co., owned by the Cowles family.

By that time I had gone to the copy desk, because I reasoned a journalist in his late 40s would have a better chance of getting hired by another paper as a copy editor, than as a reporter.

I'm going to interrupt my story about the demise of *The Courier* right here to tell you a little of my experiences on the copy desk. I'll return to the closing of the newspaper in a couple of pages. You can skip ahead, if you want.

For all my professional life, until I went on the copy desk, I had regarded editors as my enemy. Old, gray men learning English as a second language, failed dropouts from the golden ranks of reporters, in whose clumsy hands the sparkling diamond of brilliant prose was shattered beyond redemption, the novel made trite, wit changed to banality.

If copy editors were television executives, all programs would be telecast in shades of gray. They were chefs who insisted that all meals be prepared without spices. They were intruding, amateur mechanics in whose care a purring paragraph of sheer poetry was made to misfire.

I had turned down job offers to work on the copy desk from several newspapers from Portland, Oregon to New York City, but once I joined the ranks of copy editors I realized I had misjudged them. They were lapidaries who turned a rough, dull stone into a sparkling jewel.

For the most part, copy editors suffer from a bad image. There is a scene toward the end of *The Front Page* in which the star reporter bids farewell to his reporter cronies on the City Hall beat. He is leaving the profession for regular hours, a normal life and marriage. And the fate that awaits his card-playing buddies? They will end their days worn out and washed up on the copy desk.

I have seen only one copy editor portrayed on television. He turned out to be a frustrated misfit who beat his wife because he wasn't made a reporter. I missed reporting. I missed having a byline and a column. I missed being a privileged observer at events in the making and contract with influential members of the community and the world. I missed getting out of the office and the opportunity, within the restrictions of accuracy and balance, to be creative.

Sitting all day correcting grammatical and style errors and writing headlines is not a job I am temperamentally well suited to do. After a couple of years on the desk I felt my legs were growing shorter. And after they replaced our soft-leaded pencils with computers I had nightmares in which all the people were the same green shade as the screen on the monitor.

We had the first generation of Sperry-Rand computers and they were a disaster. For some reason, if too many people got on the elevator the whole system crashed. Reporters lost the stories they were working on and no copy could be sent to the composing room. The system was like a stubborn child with hurt feelings. Sometimes it wouldn't come out of its room and resume its assigned work for four or five hours.

This resulted in the newspaper running full-page ads on what were meant to be news pages depicting a boy with a bundle of newspapers shouting, "Read *The Courier-Express.*" Only those of us who knew what news stories had been intended for those pages realized the irony in the ad.

And the system was slow. Green apples have been ripened in the time it took to call up a single wire story on the screen. Sometimes when I was acting national editor, I would go to the evening conference of the various editors without AP or UPI wire copy describing major breaking events because the stories hadn't come up on the screen.

Writers and editors on the whole are notoriously inept and fumble-fingered when it comes to things that are mechanical, mathematical or electrical.

The long rows of keys caused some writers to regard the equipment as some sort of electronic sales register. One newsman spent a day punching buttons at random in an effort to open the cash drawer.

As someone who is electronically challenged, I believe that radios, television sets and computers run on actual grace. I am certain we had so much trouble with the computers because they hadn't been blessed. A generous sprinkling of Lourdes water together with magical Latin words recited by a mitered bishop might have solved our computer problems. Lacking that, computer operators would have been well advised to wear strings of garlic around their necks when sitting before the keyboard.

Such suggestions were met by editors with the same cold look a passenger on the Titanic might have gotten if he had asked the captain to take a more southerly route to avoid icebergs.

And so it befell that at a quarter to 3 on a cold Saturday morning, while working on copy intended for the early afternoon street edition, I displeased the electronic god inside the machine. I had edited a story and pushed the blue "Q-Take" button. I looked with horror at the screen as the words began to break up into random letters of the alphabet and drift downward like bright green noodles settling in the bottom of a bowl of alphabet soup.

High on the screen flashed the message: "TERMINAL EXECUTED BY THE OPERATOR."

Chapter 25

The Suit

I learned that *The Courier-Express* had been purchased by Cowles Media when I saw the headline in *The Buffalo News as* I came out of Sunday mass in the spring of 1979.

The new Cowles management was welcomed by most of the editorial staff. Cowles was then a respected and powerful name in publishing. The family had owned the lively *Look* magazine — the most liberal of the large format, mass circulation magazines, until it ceased publication in the 1960s. Cowles' holdings in the 1970s included some of the best newspapers in the U.S., its Minneapolis and Des Moines, Iowa newspapers. It had the controlling interest in the hallowed Harper & Row Publishing Co., and owned 22 per cent of the stock of *The New York Times.*

Staffers looked forward to changes that would improve the quality and circulation of the *Courier* and give the editorial department an even-tempered management.

But what began as a bright and happy beginning turned into a tense drama with an ending as inevitable and forlorn as Willie Loman's suicide in *Death of a Salesman.*

I've heard unproven reports that members of the Cowles management team said that if they were not impeded by a union contract they would have fired the entire staff when they took over the paper. Whether that was true or not, veteran journalists believed it and the attitude of the new management fostered that impression.

A new executive editor, Joel Kramer, later to become publisher of the Minneapolis Star-Tribune and still later, *The Toronto Globe & Mail,* was named executive editor, the top job in the newsroom. Kramer, 34, had been a copy editor at Newsday on Long Island.

One of his first actions was to take away the column of the city's most popular sports columnists, Phil Ranallo. Ranallo, who had written the column for 25 years, was put on the sports copy desk.

There were five managing editors during a 12-month period, starting in early 1981. The last one Judith A. Stark, 34, weekend managing editor of the Providence Journal, who was to remain until the death of the paper in the fall of the following year.

During that period, four persons held the title of Sunday editor, three held the position of sports editor. New financial, metropolitan, assistant Sunday and national editors were named. New posts were created -- editorial page editor, news editor, assistant managing editor, managing editor for features, news art director. Newly hired men and women, or staffers filled all but two of the new promotions and new management jobs with less than two years service.

New reporters were lured from other papers at a salary of $675 weekly -- about $150 more than veteran reporters at the paper were earning.

In all, there were 24 management shifts within two years, in all but one, a younger person replaced someone over 40.

The staff roster had the impermanence of the lineup of a pro football team during its first exhibition game of the season.

In going to other metropolitan newspapers for new management the C-E brought in many bright, top-drawer people. Some of the management shifts were welcomed by many of the staff. Furthermore, because they were protected by the Guild contract, none of those displaced lost pay.

Most of the changes were announced in the paper, the public told that the former editor "is returning to his first love of writing." Some editors retired, by their own choice, or under pressure.

I was no longer an officer of the Guild, but Unit Chairman Pat Ryan asked me to head a committee to investigate whether editors were being demoted because of age discrimination. The committee was comprised of men and women from both sides of the age 40 line.

When asked how I came to become involved, I sometimes replied, "I reached my middle-aged crisis and it was a question of getting a mistress or suing the paper. My wife didn't approve of a mistress."

That's not true. I'm not sure but what Ann might have preferred my keeping a mistress.

The committee hoped to avoid any legal action against the C-E in the belief it would be harmful to the paper and would create unwelcome tensions between the new management and older workers and, perhaps, between younger journalists and veteran newsmen and newswomen.

As the months went by, however, it became increasingly evident that it would be difficult to resolve the issue through talks between management and the Guild.

By mid-1981, when the committee was appointed, most of the promotions, appointments and job transfers had occurred and we recognized that as a union we couldn't ask any of the members to resign a promotion, nor could we dictate who the members of management should be.

At the same time, the union's attorney informed us that the pattern of hiring and promotions and job transfers in the past 18 months showed a prima facie case of age discrimination.

It was a legal opinion we felt we couldn't ignore. In October, after the committee's findings were reported to a meeting of the local, it was unanimously moved that the local's officers be empowered to file age discrimination complaints with state and federal agencies against the *Courier-Express*, unless the issue could be resolved at meetings between the union and management.

Only one meeting was held. At the brief November session, one of the paper's lawyers, John Taylor, said the *Courier*'s position was that it didn't discriminate and "if you asked for only a token settlement, say, of ten dollars, we wouldn't give it to you."

The following week, the Guild filed charges. The complaint was signed by me as chairman of what became known as the Over 40 Committee.

Twenty-eight persons were named as complainants. Of them, eight later asked that their names be withdrawn. At least three of the eight sent letters to management expressing their disagreement with the charges and anger at the Guild for including them in the complaint.

Two of the included distorted versions of conversations they said had been held between them and myself.

Six persons were added to the complaint at their request.

That veteran journalists at the C-E were charging age discrimination appeared prominently on the first local news page of *The Buffalo News.* It was picked up and aired on local radio stations. *The Courier* followed with a story of its own quoting staffers as former Sunday editor Doug Smith who wanted no part of the suit and said it was unfair to management. My name was in all the stories as the leader of the action.

It was painful going to work after that. When I rode up to the newsroom on fourth floor in one of the *Courier* elevators with a member of management there was silence.

It wasn't easy for someone of my generation to take legal action against my employer of 18 years. Those of us old enough to remember the Depression and World War II were not inclined to rock the boat. We had learned to respectfully wait our turn for earned rewards or life's pleasures, whether from a lover or in the workplace waiting to gain the experience and skill to advance from a smaller to a larger newspaper, to rise from rewriting handouts to a coveted and demanding beat or column, or to scale the corporate ladder.

When I began my career as a copyboy, I addressed the editors as sir. I bore no resentment when I was addressed as "boy!" by editors and reporters, a few not much older than I, even though I was an Army veteran.

It was the awful realization on the part of many of over 40 on the newspaper that, not only had we lost our turn, but also we were regarded as incompetent by the new, young, Eastern Establishment management, that was responsible for my signing the complaint of age discrimination.

Three years later the Cowles Corp. would settle the case, paying $1,400 to each of those named in the suit without admitting guilt, but by then the paper had closed its doors and many involved in the action were out of work.

Chapter 26

The Fat Lady Sings

A few minutes after midnight on the morning of Saturday, Sept. 18, 1982, the fat lady sang.

Channel 2's Tony Farina had just ended a news special on the overwhelming vote taken by Newspaper Guild members at *The Courier-Express* against accepting terms offered by publisher Rupert Murdoch for keeping the paper alive.

"The Guild members at the *Courier* have chosen to die with dignity," Farina, a former *Courier* staffer, said. The program ended on that note and the station switched to Johnny Carson, who was introducing a buxom opera singer. The introduction ended and the fat lady sang and we knew it was all over. On Sunday morning the *Courier* would be as dead as yesterday's news.

After Mass that Sunday, the last edition of the *Courier* was being sold outside the entrance of St. Peter & Paul Church in Hamburg. A woman coming out of the church glanced at the banner headline. "GOODBYE", it said. "I blame this on the unions," she sniffed.

What sort of madness would cause a union dominated by editorial employees to sign the death warrant for a major newspaper whose roots in the community went back 148 years?

I had taken an extended Labor Day weekend in 1982. I was home the day after Labor Day resting from a day at the Canadian Exposition in Toronto with my two youngest children, Jonathan, then a high school junior, and Margaret, in seventh grade.

That afternoon John Cowles Jr, head of the crumbling Cowles publishing empire, announced in the crowded *Courier* lunch room that the newspaper would fold in ten days.

I received a phone call telling me of the news from Ron Wade, the news editor at 4:15 p.m. "I have some bad news to tell you," he began.

After giving me the news, he suggested I might want to turn on my television set. Cowles was making the announcement at a hastily called press conference.

My reaction was a mixture of relief and sheer terror. Relief because my ordeal of coming to work for a company where I was no longer wanted or respected was over.

Terror because I didn't know if I would ever again work as a journalist.

I had known the paper was losing money, circulation and advertising, despite all Kramer's efforts to get bright people from other cities who would make the *Courier* more appealing to readers in Buffalo. Daily circulation was down by 4,000 from two years before. Sunday circulation had dropped by 10,000 in the same period.

No one person, or management or union can be blamed for the *Courier*'s death. Some of the causes began a couple of decades earlier, when the paper began losing circulation.

Since the late 1950s, the city the area had been losing population. In the late 1960s, it began losing industry and major retailers.

Few communities in the U.S. can support two daily newspapers. Even in New York City only one paper — the *Times* — remains healthy. In the 20 months before the *Courier* shut down its presses and closed its doors, readers in major cities had experienced the disappearance of such long time newspaper giants as the *Philadelphia Bulletin,* the *Cleveland Press,* the *Washington Star* and Cowles' own *Minneapolis Star* and *Des Moines Tribune.*

The closing of the last two papers, in particular, foreshadowed the end of the *Courier*. It signified that the Cowles empire was crumbling. In 1980, the corporation's profits dropped 37 percent. The following year they declined another 9 percent and in May 1982, profits were down an alarming 89 percent.

In 1983, Cowles Media, which had sold its stock in Harper & Row and *Harper's Magazine,* would report a half million-dollar loss.

At the beginning of August 1982, Cowles had lost the will, and maybe the ability, to keep the *Courier* alive. That's when the decision to close the paper was made in corporate headquarters in Minneapolis.

Roger Parkinson, the *Courier*'s new publisher, was one of the few persons in Buffalo who knew of the decision.

Throughout August the paper continued bringing in new faces. A new sports editor took over. A former sports writer from the *Washington Star* began covering the Bills. Two new general assignment reporters began work.

Members of the Guild retired or left the paper having no knowledge it was about to fold, thereby losing their rights to collect thousands of dollars in severance pay and unemployment benefits.

Staffers were told a new computer system would be installed in October.

A woman who was to train editorial members on the use of the new system came to Buffalo on the day it was announced the paper would close. On the same day, the family of the paper's new advertising manager arrived from Iowa and work began on a new sidewalk in front of the building.

Many employees knew the paper was in trouble, but no one expected it to close in the fall. The paper had taken its losses for the year. It would start making a monthly profit in the coming months before Christmas. It has never been satisfactorily explained why the paper would close in mid-September.

There was and continues to be a strong suspicion that the announced closing was an attempt to force the unions at the paper to agree to terms to be imposed by Rupert Murdoch, if he was to buy the paper.

Unknown to most employees of the newspaper, Murdoch had expressed a serious interest in buying the paper in August. His representatives had toured the facilities with Parkinson dressed in slacks and sport shirts to cause employees to think the publisher was showing a few out-of-town friends the plant.

In the end, Murdoch decided against the purchase.

His staff gave three reasons. At the top was the near certainty that the unions would fiercely oppose the cost cutting measures that Murdoch felt was necessary to turn the paper around.

The other reasons were that the paper was failing and the Buffalo economy was declining.

Following the announcement the paper would close, leaders of the Guild and the craft unions tried to save the paper by seeking a new publisher. I believed that any effort to rescue the paper was doomed and that the attempt would end with the unions being blamed for its demise; that is what came about.

What happened after the closing announcement was the final and wrenching chapter of *The Courier-Express,* the Murdoch chapter. It was to create an issue that divided the staff of the newspaper and left a residue of bitterness that still exists among some former employees.

Acting through Parkinson, the leaders met with Murdoch on Sept. 12 in New York City. The Australian-born magnate was given, or thought he had, assurances from the Guild and the other eight unions at the paper that he would get the concessions he desired.

The following day, a Monday, the staff was again summoned to the newspaper lunchroom on the second floor.

"This is a happier occasion than when we were here last week," Parkinson said. He introduced Donald Kummerfeld, president of Murdoch's North American arm, News America, and Robert Page, picked to be the new publisher.

Kummerfeld said Murdoch would buy the paper if the unions agreed to his demands.

The public and many *Courier* employees thought there was no alternative. I had no role in the negotiations that would follow, but I was sure the fate of the paper would depend on what demands Murdoch was making. They had not been announced and when I asked the question at the meeting in the lunchroom, Kummerfeld declined to reveal them, saying they would be kept secret until talks with the unions were over.

A deadline of midnight Thursday was set for all the unions to agree to Murdoch's terms, still unknown.

The Cowles and Murdoch people may have thought that by announcing that the paper would close in less than two weeks employees and union officials would be willing to accept any terms to keep the paper operating. That seems logical. But people are inclined to put their own self-interest and their passions above the needs of an organization.

Once it was announced that the paper would close, editorial staffers placed frantic calls to other publications asking to be hired. Reporters were spending as much time on the phone seeking jobs as they did talking to news sources.

The major activity of the newsroom staffers became to find another job. Putting out the newspaper became a secondary occupation. Although it was accomplished and done well, it was a distraction. Our main concern was how we were going to support our families and ourselves.

Many of the young reporters and editors had found jobs or had good leads by the time Murdoch's announcement was made. Many of the older employees began looking forward to an early retirement, to be made easier by state unemployment pay and contracted severance benefits amounting to as much as $50,000. They would not get those benefits if the paper continued to publish.

For most of the middle-aged employees as myself whose careers had plunged as a result of the recent change of hands, there was little likelihood that the Murdoch management would reverse our fortunes. Indeed, it was discovered when Murdoch's conditions were announced, we were likely to lose our jobs.

The Guild was willing to accept a wage cut and give up holidays. It was not willing to submit to the wholesale job slaughter asked by Murdoch: a 40 percent cut in staff regardless of seniority.

As someone who had been active in the union and had signed a complaint against the paper's management, I was virtually certain to lose my job regardless of whether the paper continued to publish or not. There were several others in the same boat.

Furthermore, Murdoch was asking that anyone fired lose their severance pay, if they accepted a job with the *News* within a year.

Not that there was much chance of being hired by the *News,* which announced it would have to make the same deep job cuts as Murdoch in order to stay in competition.

Those fired by a Murdoch *Courier* would indeed be left in the cold. Hope, now, lay with a healthy *News* that announced it would produce a morning edition, hiring former *Courier* employees, if the C-E folded.

The Guild might, for a time, save the *Courier,* but a large percentage of its members at both papers would lose their jobs. The total number of editorial jobs lost at both papers could possibly be higher if the *Courier* were to continue operating under Murdoch's terms.

So much of the decisions made in that dismal week had to do with pride, and hope and despair -- and mathematics.

It was mathematics that indicated we would save few jobs in Buffalo by agreeing to the proposed drastic cuts. It was mathematics that told realists two major newspapers could not survive in the Buffalo economy, anymore than they have been able to survive in the vast majority of U.S. cities. We, in the end, were in the middle of a deep and stormy lake knowing we could save only one of two swimmers from drowning.

The decision would ultimately be made by a vote by Guild members at the *Courier.* By that time, however, many employees had grown frustrated and angry at decisions that left our lives in turmoil and in which we had no part.

Standing in line in the Salvation Army headquarters waiting to learn how to apply for such things as unemployment benefits and food stamps, one veteran employee expressed what many were thinking: "I'm tired of having my chain pulled. We ought to tell Murdoch: 'Go to hell!'"

When the vote was made to accept or turn down Murdoch's offer, it was almost anti-climatic. The climax had come in a hotel in suburban Cheektowaga the previous night, when the Guild negotiation team turned down Murdoch's demands and his representatives stalked out of the meeting four hours before the midnight deadline they had set.

There had been only three days of talks. It was not enough time.

At the meeting held in the Hotel Sattler's Golden Ballroom the night of Friday, Sept. 17, I was among those who spoke against the offer. Perhaps what we had accomplished in the Guild were small things, I said. But we had given our members job security. The Murdoch paper would have no job security and we were unlikely to have jobs. It was better to stick together and say to hell to Murdoch as a group, than to be fired individually in a matter of a few weeks.

My speech was greeted with loud applause. When the vote came, more than 90 percent of the members raised their hands to support the Guild team with pride -- and with tears.

Unhappily for my comfort, the small minority who favored accepting Murdoch's terms included most of the copy desk staff, with whom I was to spend my final hours working at the *Courier*.

On Sept. 19, 1982, the *Courier-Express* published its last edition. Over the masthead was printed in large, red letters: Goodbye.

Chapter 27

Labor Reporter

The first time I entered *The Buffalo News* building on Washington Street in the city's downtown, was when I was president of The Buffalo Newspaper Guild. I walked in as the chief negotiator for members of the classified ad department who were having a difficult time getting satisfactory terms for their first contract.

We reached an agreement that allowed us to walk away from the table with amiable feelings all around.

The editors of the paper were familiar with the stories I had written for *The Courier-Express*. Still, it was three anxious months after the *Courier* crashed before I was hired.

Murray Light, the editor of the *News*, sent word he wanted to talk to me. "You don't have to show any clippings. We've been reading you for years," he said. It was Christmas week. I started at the *News* the day after New Year's covering education until I would replace Ed Kelly, who was retiring as paper's labor reporter after 30 years.

I think Murray Light believed the unions would welcome me as a reporter. Ed Kelly had developed a warm relationship with most union officials during three decades of covering them, although he was acidly critical of many of them in private.

I was told by a wise editor at the *Milwaukee Sentinel*, "A good reporter should never join an organization or have any friends."

I generally tried to follow that advice in my career, although, proof of my many shortcomings, I have sometimes failed.

Some of the local labor leaders welcomed me as Kelly's replacement. They regarded me as someone who would report only news and facts favorable to them.

I am a union man. I have been most of my life. Virtually every profession in America and thoughout the Western World has an organization to promote the interests and financial welfare of its members. That includes lawyers, doctors, and business owners. But when workers unite to protect and further their interests that they are looked upon by many as subverting the American way of life.

A union is simply an organization of workers who have joined together to better the conditions under which they will work and, where possible, to increase the rewards of their labor. No wise union leader or member wants to put their employer out of business and thus deprive themselves of their wages and benefits.

Nevertheless, the labor beat is the most difficult of all the beats I have covered. Many union officers and members are hostile to the press. It's common for speakers at any large gathering of union members to attack the press either for its coverage or labor or accuse it of lack of coverage.

"All you do is write about strikes," I was often told by an angry union member. Ironically, the accusation was made during a period in which many unions have lost the power to conduct an effective strike.

I was also criticized by union members for not writing more about their strike. "We've been on strike for five weeks and it's been a week since I've seen a story in the newspaper. We're readers too."

Many local union leaders and their members don't understand the role of a labor reporter. They regard him or her either as an enemy representing big corporations or as a press agent working solely for their interests. Of course, that's true of many businesses also.

I was glad to write about many accomplishments by unions. But there are a few union officials who muddy the name of honest unions. There are union leaders who have a history of suppressing democracy in their union. There are unions that have ties to organized crime. They are a small minority, thank God, but they do exist.

When a local union official and his family took in more than $300,000 annually from their various offices in unions whose members made far less than the national average wage I wrote about it.

When there was testimony at a National Labor Relations Board hearing that management had paid a union to represent its workers and appointed its officers, I wrote about it.

When unions lost a strike and their members and power declined, I wrote about it, not happily, but truthfully.

I wrote about the last steel being poured in Buffalo, about jobs going to Mexico and closing after closing of unionized plants. There are times I felt like a recorder of Irish military history, or a French balladeer at Agincourt.

There is an expression often heard in the labor movement that "Injury to one is injury to all." Some union members regarded me as a traitor to their cause. They believed I was writing such stories with the intention of damaging the labor movement. I sometimes received anonymous phone calls at home in which such accusations were made in crude language.

At a meeting of the Buffalo AFL-CIO Council a letter was read in my presence calling me "arrogant, anti-union and quite frankly ignorant." Most of the delegates enthusiastically applauded.

Chapter 28

The Last Act

Shortly before the *Courier-Express* folded, I returned to my early efforts of writing plays. In 1985, I saw a play of mine staged for the first time. It was based on the turmoil and conflicts and loss that took place in the closing days of the paper. It was called *Copy Desk.*

It was done in a small theater in downtown Buffalo. The directing was haphazard, the acting was mediocre at best and the theater was cramped and had a very rudimentary stage. But people came. They reacted. They laughed. They applauded.

I was further encouraged when the Hollywood Theatre Club put the play on in its Theatre Rapport in Los Angeles, although the experience itself was one of the worst that can befall a playwright.

I once had a nightmare in which a play of mine opened and was so trite and predictable that the audience was reciting the lines before the actors. Before the play ended, the audience burnt down the theater and tore up the sidewalk in front of it. The state legislature banned me from ever coming into California again and Congress passed a bill taking away my citizenship.

I wasn't stopped from crossing the California border and the theater wasn't torched, but the play suffered misfortunes only a little less disastrous.

The actor playing the lead quit the show the week before it was to open. The show's opening was postponed, but some critics didn't get the word and showed up at a darkened theater. That was the good part.

The bad was when I and Ann and daughter Margaret arrived in Los Angeles for the actual opening. I went to the dress rehearsal and found to my dismay that the play had been changed without either my consent or knowledge. The acting was a little better than it had been in Buffalo, but not to a marked degree.

I said nothing after the rehearsal, but I could sense the play was in trouble. There were lines in the early part of the play that had gotten laughs in Buffalo, as they were intended. The LA audience of would-be movie stars, mostly in their early 20s, invited free to attend the dress rehearsal reacted as though they were watching a staging of *Oedipus Rex* performed in the original Greek by mentally retarded patients in a nursing home.

In a bar afterward, having a drink with the cast and staff, I sat next to the director. "We appreciate the fact that you didn't object to the way we changed the play," he said.

I thought of several replies. I could have pointed out that what had been done was not only illegal and immoral, it was also wrong for the play.

I gave a small laugh meant to express bitterness, but I think it didn't have the right tone. He thought I was being a good sport.

"There's not much I can do about it now."

"It was done for the best," he assured me.

The review in *Variety* was not bad, except it called the play *City Desk*. The director and the producer had changed the lines in the script. The reviewer had changed the title. I felt I was reading a review of someone else's play.

Still I was encouraged when I read, *Copy Desk* is knowingly written and ably performed." Not exactly a rave, but far better than the assessment of the *Los Angeles Times* reviewer who wrote: "Joseph P. Ritz should send *Copy Desk* through a copy desk -- or through several of them, for as long as it takes to whip it into shape."

I thought about committing slow suicide by taking up smoking and having eggs and bacon for breakfast every morning. Still, it had been a heady feeling to see my name painted on the side of an out-of-town theater in a major city.

I've written a dozen other plays and some have been staged in small theaters in Manhattan and other places. A couple have won awards and national play contests. One, a play inspired by the love affair the poet, mystic, author and Trappist monk Thomas Merton had with a student nurse shortly before his sudden tragic death in Bangkok in 1968 was published in an anthology entitled, *INCISIONS, Award*

Winning Plays from the Stage and Screen Book Club. But the book was out-of-print the following year and Doubleday has rung down the curtain on the book club.

I still write plays and other works, but now in my 70s, I know I will never be known as a major playwright.

Chapter 29

Death of a Poet

I had been seeing my foster mother at least once a year since I had begun my career as a journalist. The visits were either in Canton or in the various places we lived since I married Ann: the small apartments in Milford, Connecticut and Yonkers and our ranch homes in New Windsor, outside of Newburgh and in Hamburg, New York.

Between her husband's pension and insurance and Social Security, she seemed to have enough to live as she always had -- frugally. She gave up selling Avon products and began writing poetry full time. A few of the poems she sold to Catholic magazines.

She had opposed Social Security in the 1930s. She still opposed it on the grounds she was afraid it would be taken away and leave her in poverty.

Characteristically she took a dark view of my career and our property, which was much larger than the converted garage and small lot in Canton.

"It's nice. I hope you'll be able to keep it," she said when she first visited our house in Hamburg and its nearly two acres of lawn and trees and flowers. She said the same thing about my job, which she suspected was a front for some sort of spy activity on behalf of the C.I.A. or some other U.S. governmental agency.

She was never comfortable with children and it was my feeling that her interest in her grandchildren was somewhat perfunctory and abstract, as though they were noisy and active visitors from a neighbor's house. But they seemed to like her, or take no notice of her indifference.

When she was 76, the doctor discovered she had breast cancer that had spread to a lung. She had an operation in Canton to remove much of the cancer, but the doctors said it was spreading to other parts of her body and she had only a couple of years to live.

Through an agent, I sold the house on Girard Avenue for $3,000. I didn't meet the family who bought it, but I was told they were black, so my mother's threat of putting a black family next to Mrs. Schario was fulfilled.

By that time, the neighborhood had many black families and I don't think it mattered much.

I took my mother to a modern, new nursing home in Batavia, New York, about 40 miles from Buffalo. The home had a pleasant staff and offered arts and crafts and games for the residents. I think she lived more comfortably than she ever had in her life. If she missed the house in Canton she never mentioned it.

She was in the nursing home only a couple of months when she fell and broke her hip and was thereafter confined to a wheelchair.

Two years later, the cancer, which had been more or less in remission since the operation, returned full-blown. I last saw her on a Memorial Day weekend. It was on a Sunday when Ann and I drove to Batavia. We found her in great pain, tossing her head from side to side from the force of the attacks and hardly able to talk. Her face had shrunken and her eyeballs bulged out of dark sockets that seemed to have deepened.

She recognized us, but could talk very little. "I can't concentrate," she whispered.

Ann held her hand for a long while in silence, then asked if she wanted us to go.

"No!" she said forcefully, a harsh, grating sound that seemed to come somewhere from deep in her chest.

We stayed another hour. I went to the nurse in charge and told her my mother was in great pain. I asked if something could be done to ease it.

"I guess the shot we gave her earlier wasn't enough," she said.

She promised to call the doctor for permission to give my mother another shot of whatever painkiller they were using.

We left soon after, promising to return in a few days.

On Memorial Day, the children and I spent the day paddling a cheap plastic raft on 18 Mile Creek, a small, shallow stream a five minute walk from our home that over thousands of years has cut a gorge more than 100 feet deep through mostly slate and shale down to what was once part of an ancient lake in the Pennsylvanian Period some 300 million years ago.

The stream is known by paleontologists as one of the world's richest sources of brachiopods and trilobites, fossils of life that lived in the water during that period.

In the afternoon, we went to where the steam broadens before emptying into Lake Erie and the children began looking for fossils while I paddled the raft aimlessly in circles.

Ann found us there about 5:45.

"It's a pretty slow trip," she said.

"I need bigger paddles."

I pulled the raft to shore and retrieved a paddle that had started to float downstream.

"The nursing home called a little after 5," she said quietly, looking down at me from the bank above. There was a note in her voice that spoke of something she was reluctant to say, a fact stuck in a tight tube that was being squeezed out by the pressure of necessity.

"The woman said your mother's health is deteriorating. They said she was much worse than Sunday."

"Oh!" I said. I started to add that I had better drive to the nursing home.

"They called back a few minutes later to say she had died."

I was shocked. My first reaction was to regret I hadn't stayed longer at her bedside the night before. I was guilty of letting her die alone among strangers.

She had been a force in my life as strong as a rushing stream that I was forced to paddle against in order to make forward progress. Although the experience had left many unhappy memories, her death had left a void.

I phoned the nursing home as soon as I got home. The woman who answered said my mother had been in a coma most of the day and had not awakened before she died.

I phoned my mother's sisters in Atlanta and Los Angeles and her brother in Austin, Minnesota. None planned to attend the funeral to be held in Canton.

Her sister in California said I had been wonderful to care for my mother in her last days and everyone was proud of me. I had really done very little except choose the nursing home and I had chosen one in New York because Canton, where her few friends were, had no nursing homes approved for Medicaid, that would pay most of the costs.

Her 82-year-old brother didn't seen upset by the news of my mother's death. He said matter-of-factly, "I thought Mae or Helen would go next." He had reached the age where death was the only important act left for those closest to him.

I phoned a funeral home in Buffalo and arranged to have my mother cremated. It was something that the Roman Catholic Church had banned in ordinary circumstances throughout most of my motherÕs and my lifetime on the grounds that the act of burning was intended to symbolize denial of the resurrection after life.

While little had been said about the dropping of burning napalm on the living during time of war, only recently had the Catholic Church approved cremation of the dead. The priest who answered the phone at St. Benedict's parish was surprised and sounded angry when I told him I was planning a cremation. He demanded to know what bishop had given permission.

"I think the undertaker got permission. He said he'd take care of everything."

"I doubt that he did. Well," he sighed regretfully, "it's too late. We've never had a cremation in this parish."

"It's my first time too."

He reluctantly agreed to a memorial mass for the dead and a private burial service at the grave attended by only the priest and I.

Officials at Calvary Cemetery were opposed to burying my motherÕs ashes in the grave I had earlier purchased next to that of her husband's body. They agreed only on the condition that the funeral notice not mention that cremains were being disposed of in their cemetery.

He need not have demanded the requirement. The Guild was striking *The Canton Repository* and it was not publishing a daily paper.

And so, when my mother was buried there was no obituary or death notice and besides my own family, the memorial mass was attended only by my father's relatives and Mrs. Schario.

That was in 1972. Since then, many of the newspapers I once wrote for, *The Detroit Times, The New York Herald-Tribune, The Newburgh News, The Buffalo Courier-Express,* have disappeared. *The New York Post* is barely holding on and may close before you read this. Newspaper readership is also declining, particularly among young adults. *The Milwaukee Sentinel* has been absorbed by *The Journal. The Gloversville Leader-Herald is* now part of a chain. Local radio news is a ghost of what it was in the 1950s and 1960s.

When I began my career as a journalist, virtually every household subscribed to a newspaper. Today, only half of the adult population regularly read a newspaper.

A few years ago I retired as a journalist for a daily newspaper, after working for 11 years on the once rival *Buffalo News.*

But I continue to write for publication, although now publication and a paycheck is no longer assured. Five of my plays have been produced in various parts of the country, including New York City. One, *Trappists,* has won some national honors under various titles and been published in an anthology of award winning plays.

I know at this late age that I will never win a Tony or the National Book Award. I know that I will never have dinner in the White House or have my book or play turned into a movie, or receive an honorary degree from an Ivy League college. And I will never live in a mansion with an Olympic-sized swimming pool.

But I still spend the majority of my days writing. You know why so many old men died when soldiers overran the Indian villages in the old days? It wasn't because they couldn't run away. They stayed for the honor of dying while they fought their enemies.

It's tempting to say that I write to make the world better, but that would be like trying to stop the earth's rotation by sticking my hand into the wind. I write knowing that I will fail and that my idea of good is not everybody's and perhaps even not shared by whoever my readers are. But I find pleasure in the argument.

Writing is my conversation with the world. It has been so since my foster mother, wanting rest and quiet, sent me to my room to write an essay on what I had done that weekend. I had just finished second grade.

It has taken me a lifetime to admit that however irrational, confused, prejudiced and paranoid she might have been, she had a major influence in how my life turned out.

It was an often painful and bewildering childhood. But then, childhood is painful and bewildering and unfair for most humans. Many children have endured far worse.

Nor do I have any lingering resentments toward my natural mother. I understand she gave me away for what must have been difficult and compelling reasons and she had no role in choosing who would raise me. For what she gave me I am grateful to her. She gave me the most important gift of all -- life.

I have tried to make the most of it.

###

Printed in the United States
70251LV00005B/174